W9-DGF-569

Here's what they're saying about Tony Bender's writing...

"...effortless ability to turn any topic he chooses into a heartwarming story. In a world filled with worrisome news and troubling times, his skill in using humor is a welcome breath of fresh air."

—Writer's Digest

"Bender writes with an uncommon blend of humor and compassion."

—South Dakota Magazine

"It's not poetry. It's better... Bender's columns are perfect. They do what a good piece should do: hook the reader right from the first words, ferrying him along till the writer is ready to set him down..."

—Grand Forks Herald

"He makes people laugh, makes people cry and makes people feel good about living in a small town."

—Aberdeen American News

"Some people just have it—a certain knack or ability to perform a certain task better than others. When it comes to writing newspaper columns, Tony Bender has it."

—Brookings Register

"Bender captures the rhythms of farming frugality and generous community spirit in his writing."

—Sioux Falls Argus Leader

I

REDHEAD

PUBLISHING, INC.

Prairie Beat

by Tony Bender

Cover design by Redhead Publishing

Edited by Jane Haas

Prairie Beat

Copyright © November 1, 2002

by Tony Bender

All rights reserved. No part of this book, either in part or whole may be reproduced, transmitted or utilized in any form or by any means, electronic, photographic or mechanical, including photo-copying, recording, or by any information storage and retrieval system without permission in writing from the publisher, except for brief quotations embodied in literary articles and reviews. For permission please contact the publisher at the address below.

International Standard Book Number
0-9705442-4-3

Published by:

Redhead Publishing
119 West Main Street
Ashley, ND 58413

1-701-288-3531

redhead@drtel.net
www.ashleynd.com
www.wisheknd.com
www.tonybender.com

Printed in the United States of America

Foreward

by Jim Hornbeck

L aughter is the best medicine.

True or false?

It's true, with a caveat: Tony Bender.

The Surgeon General has warnings on cigarette packages that "Smoking can cause cancer, emphysema, burned fingers, athlete's foot, sleepwalking and other assorted maladies."

Maybe that's not word for word what the SG wrote, but forgive me. Government warnings have a way of causing my mind to vapor-lock. I'm sure the "other assorted maladies" were listed, too, but I can't remember them all. Anyway, you get the idea... some things are hazardous to a person's health.

So, I think the American Health Association should print on

the covers of Tony's books, in 72-point type (that's really big type used in headlines like the *Chicago Cubs Win World Series* or *Senator Tells the Truth*) that "Reading Bender's stories can cause self-asphyxiation from absolutely uncontrollable laughter and rug burns from rolling on the carpet in fits of hysteria. There also have been unconfirmed reports of blown lungs." Tony is one of the finest practitioners of a rare form of masochism known as humor writing. And his readers laughingly feel his pain.

He greatly admires Dave Barry. For good reasons.

Not only is Barry a talented and funny writer, he also won a Pulitzer Prize for commentary about a dozen years ago. Not George Will not Robert Novak not David Broder. All fine, serious writers of opinion columns that read like the instructions for "easy-to-assemble" child's toys of 557 pieces. No, it went to a humorist.

Somehow, a group of judges realized that writing humor is difficult, draining and demanding, all words that aren't funny. Finally, the bastard child of writing, humor, got the recognition it deserved.

Thankfully, there have been many newspaper contest judges over the years who have recognized Tony's superior craftsman-ship. In North Dakota Newspaper Association contests for best column, Tony has received first place eleventy-twelve times. (Eleventy-twelve means "a lot.") He has also been honored by the National Newspaper Association for best humor column the past two years.

Barry is good. But, I think Bender is a tad better.

Good humor writing is not always going for the big "har-de-har-har." Tony can write the "laugh-til-you-hurt" stuff better than anybody.

But he can also write the whimsical, chuckling kinds of stories in which he uses his imperfections to help us laugh at ours.

Of course, Tony's list of imperfections is rather lengthy.

His wife, "The Redhead," tried to alphabetize them once, but quit after the letter "L" because she had already used a ream of paper.

I'm not a Surgeon General or a Surgeon Sergeant, for that matter, so you likely won't obey this warning: "Read and laugh at your own risk. If you rupture a kidney laughing, it's your own damn fault. You were warned. If, while driving to work some morning, you remember one of these stories and are overcome with giggles causing you to plunge into a culvert and wrap the steering-wheel around your neck, it's your own damn fault. You have been warned by the Surgeon Corporal of the American Health Association."

—Jim Hornbeck is the marketing director for the Arizona Newspaper Association, an award-winning columnist and contributor to Chicken Soup for the Soul books.

A rebuttal

I hadn't planned to write a foreward for this book. My plan was to let someone else do the work. But after reading what Hornbeck wrote, I kinda felt like I had to defend myself. First of all, I've never considered my work life-threatening. I have, however, been threatened a time or two for things I have written. The chest heaving, vein-popping, tooth-grinding sort of threats. Maybe that's what Jim meant.

I consider it an achievement of the highest sort if I can cause someone to blow milk out of his nostrils. But no one ever died from it. Relax. The chances are good you'll live through this book. Unless you're a really slow reader.

The thing about *Prairie Beat* that pleases me the most is that it is more heavily weighted toward humor. I have long suspected that I am part Irish because when someone drops dead around me—*not from milk in the nostrils, mind you*—I feel the compulsion to eulogize them. And those tributes often were included in the collections because the writing was sincere—and some of the best I've ever done. The funerals are bad enough. Then there are fewer friends and relatives around to buy the book! Thankfully, each collection has had fewer goners than its predecessor. Hey, that might be a marketing slogan. *"Now with fewer dead folks!"*

You'll find a corpse or two littering the pages, but mostly this book reflects a satisfaction with my station in life. The joy of family. Bemusement at the world around me. And a few satiric snarls at the idiots infiltrating my life.

This humorous approach will no doubt irritate my friend Gare Bare, who insists that I'm "not that damn funny" and that I should stick to writing the cry-in-your-beer stuff. Some folks aren't happy unless they're unhappy.

That anything gets written at all is a bit of a miracle in itself considering I type with just two fingers. (Although sometimes I throw in a thumb on the space bar.) This is really not the fault of Mary Ann Nelson, my high school typing teacher. She tried. But the fact that I was seated next to Ron "Squirrel" Carlsen doomed me. He was a poor typist and driven by envy toward those of us with unlimited typing potential. Every time I got going good, he'd smash his hands down on my keyboard. I turned in a lot of speed tests which read: *snacc;iuhws'hOZ"-#XC%hbid;uOH;+U*

A guy can't really learn to type when mostly you're concerned about self defense. On the other hand, I can type about as fast as I think, so it hasn't slowed me down much.

—*Tony Bender*

IX

Dedication

There are many friends along the way who have cleared paths for me and offered friendship. They deserve my thanks. There are those, more rare in number, who have offered unwavering loyalty, and they know who they are. Bless you. And I must acknowledge the guardian angels who regularly deflect the boulders which might smash me. I don't believe in coincidence. Nor in luck.

I dedicated *Loons in the Kitchen* to my wife and children. What kind of life would I have without them? *The Great and Mighty Da-Da* was dedicated to my father and grandfathers for the grit they passed on to me. *Prairie Beat*, which reflects the joy I find in life, is dedicated to the one who taught me by example that life is to be lived large. Laughter is mandatory. If you can't beat 'em, laugh at 'em. Or laugh with them.

This is dedicated to you, Mom, for teaching me to appreciate the joy around me. I don't suppose it was a lesson you consciously taught, but it was one I learned from you just the same. I saw the way you dealt with the good days and the hard ones—with laughter.

So now I, too, smile at the sunrise. I take the time to watch the full moon rising. I grin at the freckles on my son's nose, at the toddler waddle of my daughter. They do not understand why I am smiling, but they smile back just the same. I guess maybe I'm just passing it on. Life is magic. Joy is around us, and we can always make more. Thanks for letting me in on the secret, Mom.

Table of Contents

FLAWS AND FOIBLES

CONSUMER REVOLT

FRIENDS INDEED

PRAIRIE BEAT

THE WRITE STUFF

THE OLD MAN AND THE ME

OUT OF MY LEAGUE

TRAVELIN' MAN

PRAIRIE FOLK

RELATIVELY SPEAKING

FLAWS AND FOIBLES

Reasonably functional
for a moron

I rationalize.

I rationalize that at 43 I am not losing my mind just because on a monthly basis I conduct a 10 minute search for my keys with those very same keys in my hand or that I spend a good five minutes sometimes, dismantling the bed looking for my glasses which I fell asleep wearing and are still perched firmly upon my nose.

Even though I used to remember everything, I rationalize that the reason I can't remember anything now is that I have much more to remember. I could probably still recite the box score of game six of the 1975 World Series, memorized when I was 16, but nowadays I can't even recall how old I am. (I had to research it for this column. I called my Mom. I still remember her number but for the life of me, I can't remember where she moved. She probably didn't give me the address.)

Sunday, as I headed out the door for a few hours to do some work in our Wishek office, The Redhead asked me to pick up a gallon of milk. "Oh, and we're out of toilet paper and..." (something else. I've forgotten already.)

"I'd better make a list," I said. So I made a list. For three items! It's not that I am incapable of remembering three items; it's that I am incapable of remembering three items and navigating the 15 miles to Wishek. I would expend so much brain power committing the three items to memory, I might forget where the heck I am going and what I am supposed to do once I get there.

Don't get me wrong. I am reasonably functional as morons go. Every weekday morning I remember Dylan's backpack, his jacket, his mittens, his hat and India's diapers and snowsuit. After I drop them off at school and daycare, respectively, I drive the 12 miles back home to get my briefcase. Then I put on some pants.

Let me tell you how pathetic my life has become. Every day at the office I have to spend the first 10 minutes making a list of things to do. Later in the day I will spend another 20 minutes looking for the list.

Life in a small town newspaper is harried. It's bad enough that my staff (What's Her Name and You Know) see me bumbling, barely functional, through the work day. But eventually, I am forced to communicate with the outside world and reveal I have the attention span of a gnat.

If I call someone on a crucial, pressing issue and the phone rings more than twice, the conversation often goes something like this:

"Hello?"

"Umm. Hello... Uhh... Who's this?"

"Jack." (Doesn't ring a bell.)

"So, Jack, How's the wife?"

"Still dead."

The other day, I called Allan Burke, editor of the Linton paper. Or he called me. I can't remember exactly. The point is, I am fairly certain that we did have a conversation in which we decided he would ride with me to Bismarck since we both had business there.

"What time should I be ready?" he asked.

"For what?" I responded.

Despite the fact we both had full agendas, the day went smoothly and I didn't lose my list 'til late afternoon. We both made it to our respective appointments. We dropped off his printer for repair. I picked up The Redhead's rings which were being sized at the jewelry store. We bought the special Hummus and Jerusalem sandwiches at the Green Earth Cafe for my wife. He purchased his office supplies.

Finally, we were in Wal-Mart to pick up the new Power Ranger as ordered by my son. I was weaving through the aisles, Allan in tow, when he stopped me.

"After this we need to go to Wal-Mart, right?"

I had to think about it for a moment. Then I looked up at a sign to make sure.

"We are in Wal-Mart," I said.

Poor bastard is only 53.

© Tony Bender, 2001

Writer's note: I got an e-mail from Allan the next day. He thanked me for letting him ride along to Bismarck. "But I am a little disappointed we never got to go to Wal-Mart," he wrote.

Left blinker
eternally on

ccording to official statistics, a startling number of North Dakota drivers are older than some of the things I have in my refrigerator. Some of them actually witnessed, first hand, the stuff that happened in the Bible. For example, I know a guy, Herman Leviticus, who claims to have written part of the Old Testament. But I have my doubts. Who ever heard of the Book of Herman?

But my point is, many North Dakota drivers are old. Some, in fact, are clinically dead. I am fairly certain I saw Ted Williams turning left on red in Bismarck just last week. Now, I'm not complaining about old people. I fully anticipate being one someday if the codgers don't rise up and surround my office with pitchforks and torches after the publication of this column. As I understand it, the guy who invented fire still lives around here.

Let's face it. There comes a time when you have to take away the keys. It's for your own good. Recently, one North Dakota man mistook the bay of a car wash for his garage and when he exited the vehicle, was drowned in a flurry of pink suds. Then, because the corpse was Simonized, it kept sliding right out of the coffin. The pallbearers dropped him three times on the way up to the front of the church.

In Ashley one day, I was watching as four elderly drivers met with their blinkers pointing various directions at the intersection near McIntosh County Bank. Having four cars reach the intersection simultaneously had never happened before in the history of Ashley, and none of the drivers knew who had the right of way. They stayed there, befuddled, until they ran out of gas and had to be towed away by Bobby Delzer.

Another problem with elderly drivers is they drive old cars with doors so long and heavy, when they fling them open, they inflict door dings so grievous, I was able to convince my insurance agent that I had been broadsided by the train. I almost pulled it off until someone pointed out that Burlington Northern doesn't run through town anymore.

I'm not suggesting that our elderly drivers should have to pass drivers tests or anything that revolutionary, but I think there should be a few simple rules.

If you are regularly being passed by riding lawn mowers (and some push mowers) in town, you must immediately surrender your keys.

If there is a block-long parade of cars following you down the

8

highway at 14 miles an hour, all afraid to pass because your left blinker has been on since D-Day, you must pull over and cease driving.

If you have a bobble head Chihuahua in the rear window of your Desoto, and it doesn't bobble when you drive, you must put it in park forever.

I know there will be all sorts of complaints and statistics cited after this column comes out. I'll hear how teenagers are actually more dangerous behind the wheel than senior citizens.

I agree and have a few simple rules to keep teenagers off the road as well.

If I have my way, I will make it illegal to drive any vehicle in which the stereo system is louder than the muffler. And another thing. I demand they get a new song. It is a well-known fact that all teenagers listen to the same song. The lyrics go something like this: "Boom Boom BOOM Boom BOOM! (I think it's Mozart.)

If Middle East despots ever get their hands on American speaker technology, we are sunk.

I also intend to see to it that no teenager with more chrome in his tongue than on his bumper be allowed behind the wheel. Just as a matter of principle. The same goes for those who have more tattoos than pin stripes.

And can you imagine what today's teenagers will be like behind the wheel when they get old?

We have to stop them now.

© Tony Bender, 2002

Old folks
shouldn't drive

In last week's column, which caused a furor, I suggested
that old people are bad drivers. What was I thinking? What
I meant to say is old people have no sense of humor.

For instance, after the column came out, Millard Snerdsack,
who is, as Willard Scott might say, 107 years young, got so
incensed, he rammed the building next door with his 1967
Rambler. Which may or may not prove my point. There's an outside chance it was a warning shot.

Relax. The hardware store is fine. So is the Rambler. In fact,
it took Millard three tries before he got the Rambler to jump the
curb.

I would like to point out to Tipper Gore that polka music was
blaring on the Rambler's radio, which to my mind is every bit as
dangerous as anything Ozzy Osborne ever did and should con-

tain warning labels if not be banned entirely.

Then Gottlieb Joachim came in to chew me out. "That ad in the paper made me so mad!" (Around here, anyone over 70 uses the word "ad" to describe anything in the newspaper.)

"Well, tough noogies, you old coot," I said.

"I ought to teach you a lesson, you young whippersnapper!" he said, rolling up his sleeves.

"Yeah, right, Grandpa," I said. "You and what army?"

"Punk, you couldn't last three rounds with me!" Gottlieb said.

Huh. That goes to show you how much he knows.

It was a left hook that dropped me in the second round. When I came to, Gottlieb was sitting on my chest sticking blades of grass up my nostrils. He wouldn't let me up until I listened to the story of how he had to walk to school four miles everyday, uphill both ways in a raging blizzard after milking 17 cows by hand.

"C'mon Gottlieb," I said. "It didn't blizzard every day."

"Who you gonna believe?" Gottlieb said to the gathering crowd, "Me or a guy with grass up his nose?"

If it hadn't been time for Gottlieb's morning coffee break, I might have been stuck there all day. Every weekday at 9:30 a.m. and 2:30 p.m., retired men gather at the cafe to take a break from taking a break. They can get a good dozen men around the table, all in feed store hats with a combined age of 1,404 years. They stopped having birthday cakes when the old cafe burned down.

11

We have three funeral homes in the county, and the competing undertakers used to sit at one table playing "Rock, Paper, Scissors" to see who could claim the next body. But they made them leave because they were making the customers nervous.

Once when Elmo Bzrek nodded off during coffee break, all three undertakers did "scissors" and there was a big ugly brawl. One of the undertakers was killed when the salad bar fell on him, and there was another big fight between the surviving undertakers to see who got the funeral.

Then Elmo woke up, stepped over the body of the undertaker and around the police, paid his 75 cents (no tip) and left in his Studebaker after door-dinging the car next to him.

So I guess you can't blame old folks around here for being a mite touchy, but I don't think that should excuse rudeness. Like the time the newspaper botched coverage of the Big Hat Show, and a little old lady stuffed a potato in my tailpipe. But I should point out it was peeled and nicely seasoned.

Bessie McKitrick got pretty mad about last week's column, too. Real mad. She came in to cancel her subscription four times, shaking her fist at me each time. At least I think she was shaking her fist at me. It might have been the palsy.

Sometimes we torture the elderly by running a subscription special. We offered five dollars off on a two-year subscription, and the clinic had a run on check-ups. Our frugal elderly really wanted to save $5, but the thought that they might not live that long created quite a quandary.

It's not that they fear dying. Heck, when you're 109, you see the Grim Reaper driving by and you try to flag him down. No, the dilemma is that if they die with a few months remaining on their subscription, they're going to feel cheated.

For a long time, we delivered as many as 17 papers to the Lutheran cemetery, but it made quite a mess, and the caretaker got an injunction.

But none of this really has anything to do with the purpose of this column which is to apologize profusely for suggesting that some centenarians ought to have their licenses revoked.

The truth is, they are very good drivers. That is why they refuse to drive anything that doesn't have a hood ornament. Because a hood ornament allows them to line up perfectly with the yellow center line.

There. I said it. I'm sorry. It won't happen again.

© Tony Bender, 2002

Hair's
the deal

I have confidence in my marriage; otherwise, I would not breech this topic.

There are rules with women. They never look fat even when they ask and even when they look fat.

Silence is just as deadly as saying the wrong thing. If you usually tell her she looks great when she emerges from the bathroom after six hours of primping which will put you a fashionable three hours late for a two hour movie, be consistent. If you do not tell her she looks great, she will process the omission to mean that she does not look great. Either that, or you have not noticed at all what she looks like, and that is even worse. You insensitive cur!

It's all right to say you don't like a dress. That is to say it will not doom the relationship entirely if things have been going fine to that point. Of course "fine" is in the eye of the beholder. A man may believe things are going swell. He will sit there in his underwear, scratching his belly, cheering for the Twins (Barbie) in front of the big screen, and she will sit down beside him and say, "We have to talk." But that's a whole 'nother slippery slope. My point, begun several paragraphs ago, is that you can say you do not like a particular dress—but not because it makes her look fat! You can only say you don't like the dress, however, while she is trying it on in the store. Once the dress has been purchased (on sale and non-returnable) you may not say an unkind word. Like "It makes your hips look so wide, you may have to go through the door sideways."

Besides, if you diss the dress, she will just go out and spend more on another dress that might be worse than the first. It is better to conserve your cash and let her go out dressed like a freak. But walk a ways behind her, so no one knows she's with you. You can duck down at the red lights. "Oh look, honey, is that a penny down on the floor mat?"

Another thing you never talk about is makeup. Here's the deal. Never, under any circumstances, comment on any woman's makeup. Even if she's got so much blush on she looks like she's having a massive coronary, do not comment on her red face. Even if she might really be having a heart attack, it is better to let her die than to embarrass her by performing mouth to mouth. Unless she's really cute. Then it might be worth a shot.

The thing with women and makeup is, you are not supposed

to notice that they are wearing it at all. That's getting harder all the time. Once, I started screaming at a salad bar because a woman's eyelash fell into my three bean salad, and I thought it was a spider.

It is better not to notice that she has painted bizarre green rings around her eyes. Act like it is normal for a woman to look like a raccoon. If she is wearing the pasty, white goth makeup, do not refer to her as Morticia. Just smile and pretend she does not frighten you.

Now, women have taken to wearing glitter. Even that, you must pretend to notice (but not to notice). "Darling, you are positively radiant (possibly radioactive)!"

The biggest no-no is hair. You must always notice when your sweetie changes her hair and you must always love it. But be careful. To love the new hairstyle too much might get her to thinking that her last new hairstyle was freakish—and the chances are that it was—and she may fall into a depressive funk and stop washing your socks.

It is best not to say too much. Do not say, "I love it. You look just like that guy from Lynyrd Skynrd!" Just tell her she looks great.

One time, The Redhead decided to color her hair on Super Bowl Sunday. Either she botched the job or she thought the Vikings were playing. My mistake was telling her purple was not a good look for her. She refused to go to the party. In fact, she refused to go to work until she could go to a professional and get it fixed. So we compromised. We stayed home and watched

Home and Garden TV.

While you must notice your wife has changed her hair—in fact it's in the bylaws—you almost never should risk commenting on another woman's hair. Especially if they have changed their hair completely.

This rule does not apply to men. For reasons that remain a mystery to me, I allowed a stylist in Sioux Falls to add blond highlights to my hair last weekend. It cost me $59, and then she sold me $732 in hair care products crucial to maintaining my look, including a product called Bed Head (The funky gunk that rocks).

Wouldn't you know, two old high school buddies, whom I haven't seen in five or six years, decided to take a detour from Pollock where they apparently had caught their limit of empty Budweiser cans, which were rattling around in the boat. They decided it was imperative at that exact moment in time to visit their old friend Bones and his liquor cabinet.

I opened the door. It was Woof and Whitey and a designated driver.

"What the hell happened to your hair?" Woof asked.

"At least he has hair," Whitey pointed out.

So apparently it is legal for a man to talk about another man's hair. Let's face it. Any guy willing to sit in a room with a whole bunch of women wearing a rubber hat under a hair dryer is pretty much fair game.

(For no other reason than to document it as a matter of his-torical record, I would like to point out that Woof threw up in my yard.)

But as I was saying, never, ever reveal to the world that a woman has changed her hair color. But what are rules if they are not made to be broken? As I said, I have confidence in the stability of my marriage. (Honey, if you're reading this, trust me. You don't look fat.)

Anyway, The Redhead has this silly idea that I have a thing for well-endowed blondes. I'm not admitting to anything. I will say, if the positions were reversed and mice tried to trap men, that is what they would put in the trap.

Well, little by little, she began lightening her hair. (I'm not commenting on the well-endowed part because no man's marriage is that solid.)

Then she bought a ponytail. Yup, they have ponytail shops in the mall. The thing is, she decided the hairpiece was still a bit blonder than she was. So she decided to lighten her hair even more.

At this point, it started to affect my business. I have built a career writing about The Redhead. When I started showing up at speeches with a foxy blonde on my arm, little old ladies, presuming the worst, took offense, and book sales plummeted. So you see, exposing this is really a sound business decision.

The rest of this is simply a malicious voyeuristic aside based purely on my confidence in my relationship.

The other day, after North Dakotans were surprised by the never-before recorded phenomenon of 60 mph winds, The Blondehead went to the restroom to check her makeup and discovered that she had been walking around most of the morning with no ponytail. It had blown off somewhere on Wishek's Main Street. If something like that landed in your three bean salad, it would really freak you out.

Fear not. She has another hairpiece. She slammed it in the car door the other day and it came off. It's OK to chuckle a little when that happens to your wife. But what if it happens to a total stranger?

My step-dad, Jim, was walking in the Wal-Mart parking lot in Aberdeen that windy day, when he noticed a brownish, rodent-sized clump of hair rolling on the pavement, followed by a tottering old woman who was rapidly losing ground.

Jim scooped it up like a shortstop, and then, because he has been around the block a time or two, he handled the situation like a champ considering the circumstances.

It would have been easy for him to say something stupid. Instead he just thrust it at her and said, "Here." The embarrassed woman thanked him profusely and plopped the hair back on her head sideways.

"You look great," Jim said. Then he walked back into the store and scrubbed his hands with disinfectant soap.

© Tony Bender, 2002

The whole tooth about South Dakota

Disconcerting things. I've been reading disconcerting things.

The problem is I lost the newspaper article, so I am forced to recount what clearly are indicators of the demise of civilization as we know it, purely from memory.

This from a man who once had to hire a gumshoe to find his car in the mall parking lot on a Saturday.

But let me say with complete certainty that there was an article in, uh, some newspaper, that stated unequivocally that according to people who study such things, South Dakotans brush their teeth less than citizens of any other state.

In fairness, it should be noted that Tennessee was disqualified because no one in the hill country actually had any teeth, and it threw the whole survey askew. And results from Arkansas were thrown out because when faced with answering the question, "How many days do you go between tooth brushings," 83 percent answered, "brown."

So obviously, there are serious questions about the veracity of the study. So from this point on, I'll use disclaimers like "allegedly" and "reportedly" and "possibly" and "according to a high level source who wished to remain anonymous" because that is what all irresponsible left-leaning journalists do when we want to create widespread public panic.

According to top-level secret statistics that I made up because I am desperate to somehow come up with the 700 words I need for my column this week, a full 17 percent of the population and nearly everyone from Conde, SD, brush only when the Packers win the Super Bowl.

Reportedly, (see how slick that works?) officials at the Halitosis Institute of America have donned the same outfits they wear to open anthrax-tainted mail and have rushed to Mt. Rushmore where an entire tour bus was overcome with a retching, vile illness due to airborne contamination from the ticket-taker, Mary Sue Ellen Snerdsack.

"It's not like that hasn't happened before," said a high-level HIA official who wished to remain anonymous, "but when we discovered the bus was loaded with Parisian tourists, we got concerned. Real concerned. I mean, how bad does a stink have to be to offend the French?"

After extensive interrogation, it was discovered that

Snerdsack, a die-hard Packer fan did not even brush in 1997, when the Packers beat the New England Patriots in Super Bowl XXXI (after which there was widespread panic, rioting and looting in Langford when the Cenex station ran out of tarter-control Crest).

Reportedly, Snerdsack is holding out until her demand to have Vince Lombardi autograph her left breast is met.

Snerdsack is said to be resting comfortably and under heavy sedation at an undisclosed location after being informed of Lombardi's death.

A statement released by the distraught Snerdsack family read, "We guess Mary Sue Ellen thought the death of Lombardi was a hoax, just like the man walking on the moon thing. We're not even going to tell her about Elvis."

Reportedly, a source close to the investigation allegedly said, on the condition of anonymity, that although Snerdsack has refused thus far to brush her teeth, government psychologists have succeeded in negotiating down from Lombardi. "But she's holding out for Bart Starr."

The source goes on to say that Starr, a man known for his moral convictions, has refused to consider Snerdsack's demands.

"Gee, you'd think the guy would bend a little," the source said. "After all, we have a bus load of French people throwing up in the viewing area."

But there is hope for resolution in the standoff, according to another high level government source who was interviewed off the record: "I hear we may be able to get Ringo Starr."

There you go folks. That's my report. Now I know all you South Dakotans are going to be riled up about all this and complain that I'm besmirching the good name of your state just because I live in North Dakota. Well, I was going to write about that survey recently released by the Sheepherders Union out in Helena, but Montana refused to return my call. And I haven't actually seen the report, and reporting on something without having all the facts—now that would be downright irresponsible.

Besides, as a former South Dakotan, (I was kidnapped and forced to endure slave labor) I know for a fact that some folks there don't brush their teeth.

Like my former friend Gare Bare, for example. Once, when we were kids, Gare Bare decided to see how long he could go without brushing his teeth. The experiment nearly ended with tragic results when our Cub Scout troop got lost in a shelter belt outside of town. We decided to use the moss on his teeth to find north but he kept turning and we ended up in North Platte.

But things could be worse. I understand there's a growing movement in Bemidji where some folks refuse to brush their teeth until the Vikings win the Super Bowl.

© Tony Bender, 2002

My freakishy large head

I didn't know I was a freak and that's what hurts. I had breezed through forty years unaware of my affliction but now the comfortable shroud of ignorance has been lifted.

It all started on a whim. The Redhead was at a doctor's appointment, and I was kicking around the mall when I decided to get new glasses.

My prescription hadn't been updated in four or five years and I was getting mighty close to street signs before I could read them clearly. That led to a lot of U-turns and missed exits. So for the sake of fuel efficiency, I decided to get new glasses.

The optometrist confirmed my suspicions. I am one step away from bifocals.

Prescription in hand, I marched to the front of the store where two dapper young gentlemen helped me pick out new frames.

At first, I wanted to just have the new lenses put in my existing frames. But The Redhead, who had arrived in the nick of time, chided that my old frames were decidedly out of fashion.

Besides, one of the young men added, it would cost seventy million kabillion dollars (according to the new math I have learned from my son) to do that. With the store special, for twenty bucks more, I could get *two* pair of glasses.

Fine. I don't have the patience to pick out a pair of shoelaces when we're shopping. Now I would have to pick out *two* pair of glasses.

I picked out one frame that looked suspiciously like the ones I was wearing but was informed by The Redhead that they were "old man glasses."

The salesman put another pair on my face. "What do you think?"

"I don't know," I replied. "Can't see without my glasses."

This explains why you see so many folks walking around in freaky eye wear. They all picked out glasses without being able to see. A guy getting new glasses has about as much of a chance of getting it right as Stevie Wonder at his colored sock drawer.

To complicate matters, not one of the frames I picked fit my face. Every one was too small.

"Who decides what is in style, anyway," I groused.

"College kids," I was told. College kids with baggy pants, flat abdomens, dreadlocks and skinny faces.

Finally, after half-a-dozen tries, I half kidded in exasperation,

"Gee, do I have some sort of mutant big head?"

The room went silent.

Very silent. One of the clerks looked away uncomfortably. The other studied his shoes.

And then I knew.

My Lord, it was true! I do have a freakily-large mutant big head! That explains the recent offer from Michael Jackson to purchase my bones for display alongside the elephant man.

In the embarrassing silence, I was led away to the HMC (Humongous Mutant Cranium) Collection in the corner.

There we found two pair that fit and met with The Redhead's approval. Very modern, tiny little lenses and frames wide enough to fit the grill of a Chevy Tahoe.

I'm getting used to the idea of being a mutant. Now I understand the stares of small children on the street.

But I am at peace because I know the styles will change again, and lenses the size of dinner plates will someday be back in style. The lenses will be so large, they will come equipped with wiper blades.

I will look so cool.

© Tony Bender, 2001

And our gas mileage
has improved

She was fed up. No pun intended. After two kids and mucho poundo el gaino, The Redhead had had enough. She decided we were both going to get in shape.

Lord knows I needed it. To show solidarity during her pregnancies, I had gained weight, too, going from portly to porky.

Even a 12-step program had not gotten me to set aside my liver sausage addiction; though, I admitted I was powerless over liver sausage and that my grocery bill had become unmanageable.

I was mainlining the stuff direct from the sausage stuffer, selling Dylan's Power Rangers on the street to get more black market liver sausage. I was out of control.

The Redhead suggested we try hypnotism. She's lost 55 pounds and is off the charts on the Foxy Index. I have lost 65 pounds and now am merely portly. And we have been getting better gas mileage.

By July, I had dropped more than 30 pounds, but folks around here couldn't figure out what was different. They would look at me questioningly, knowing something had changed and yet were unable to figure it out.

"You got a haircut."

"You shaved."

"You got new glasses."

When the liver sausage business in McIntosh County began to flounder, requiring federal grants to prop up the vital industry, folks began to put two and two together.

When full page ads in a large daily newspaper appeared, featuring The Redhead's endorsement for the hypnotist, the secret was pretty much out.

People find it fascinating that hypnotism could convince a guy to cut back on the lard sandwiches but it has.

It's all been a very positive experience except now the lard industry is on the verge of collapse, and the kuchen lobby is becoming desperate. They're hanging around the schools, slipping the kids free samples of prune kuchen. And they're still using a cartoon camel—Joe Kuchen—to give kids the idea that kuchen use is really cool.

On the other hand, you see public service commercials from R. J. Kuchens on the community access channel, where up to three teenagers a year have been known to tune in, advising kids that no matter how cool and fun kuchen use may appear to be, it would be best to wait until you are of legal age before destroying your body with unfettered kuchen abuse.

I was thinking of doing an expose' on the whole thing but The Redhead reminded me of all the advertising dollars the liver sausage and kuchen industries spend with our newspapers. So I have decided to compromise. I am advising folks to use "chewless" kuchen. Just a pinch between the cheek and gum eases that custard urge.

But getting back to hypnotism. Folks wonder, are there any adverse effects of, say, the Manchurian Candidate variety?

No, the only concerns I have are my sudden urges to do laundry and dishes. But I suspect The Redhead slipped them a few extra bucks to plant that seed. That and my almost uncontrollable desire to vote Republican are the only real drawbacks that come to mind.

We have had to find more closet space now that we have stopped using the treadmill to hang clothes on, but it is a minor inconvenience.

Hypnotism has helped convince us to eat smarter. The Redhead has gone pretty much vegetarian which out here in cattle country has led to some ugly incidents involving mobs with pitchforks and torches.

I, however, believe in moderation. I fear that by eating just vegetables, I will create a green bean shortage or a run on the lettuce at the produce counter. So every few days, I get the urge for meat, and some animal must die.

© Tony Bender, 2001

Editor's Note: The Redhead was featured on the cover of the Oct. 1, 2002 Woman's World Magazine. The headline read: *Reach your dream weight by programming your brain for weight loss! She did it and now she's 65 lbs slimmer!* The cover also included pictures of cookies, cupcakes and chocolate cake.

CONSUMER REVOLT

My insurance company has me over a barrel

According to the the Tax Foundation, the average American will work until April 27 to pay his or her taxes or, in the case of Rupaul, *its* taxes.

I for one, would like to boldly assert that working 116 days each year to pay taxes to my beloved Internal Revenue Service seems like a pittance. In fact, I think we should send a tip—fifteen percent minimum.

Now some folks might suspect I might be sucking up to the IRS to avoid prosecution for listing the survivors in my aquarium as dependents or that trip to *Dominatrix Helga's Leather and Handcuff Emporium* as a research expense.

Let me swear on a stack of 1040s right now that is just not so. Besides, I recently discovered that compared to insurance companies, the IRS are pikers.

The Redhead and I almost found ourselves uninsured last month when a bill from our insurance company went ignored as we played our usual game of dare to see who would flinch first and pay the bill.

Once, neither of us backed down and DirecTV cut us off just before kickoff. Faced with the loss of *Cartoon Network*, Dylan ran away from home to a friend's who not only guaranteed uninterrupted service but a Nintendo as well. We miss our son. But when he learns to write, we are confident he will send us a letter demanding his allowance.

But getting back to this insurance debacle. The Redhead had looked at the bill but concluded that since she had paid approximately $17,000 in December, we should be covered until June when we would have to sell another quarter of land to pay the bill.

As it turned out, the $17,000 covered only three months. I am not going to suggest that my sedate and demure wife slammed down the phone, snarling and cursing and swearing vengeance, but let me say that after she was done snarling and cursing, she began the search for cheaper insurance.

That is when we discovered that of the 9,659 auto insurance companies that once served our state, all but two left because they were forced under some sort of recently discovered obscure law, to actually pay claims. This proved devastating when a June hail storm completely leveled Bismarck, an event rivaled only by the Vesuvian destruction of Pompeii in 79 A.D. Underpasses were flooded with ice ten feet deep. Roofs were destroyed. Every vehicle not parked in a bomb shelter was pelted like Nixon's limo in South America. This came on the heals of the flooding in 1997 which destroyed Grand Forks and washed Fargo downstream.

So if you have not been to North Dakota in some time, that is why Reeder is now the state capital and the second-largest city in the state.

According to official reports, insurance companies in North Dakota suffered a 297% loss ratio which means after you consider the usual 700% profit ratio, insurance companies will be forced to suffer through only a 403% profit margin.

This has also devastated the wheelbarrow rental industry because the insurance companies will require fewer wheelbarrows to haul their profits out of the state.

These natural disasters have overwhelmed the insurance industry in other ways, too. Insurance adjusters, lonelier than the Maytag repairman, were suddenly forced to take a crash course in filling out claim payments.

The volume of claims also overwhelmed the check-writing department (a gal named Betsy who comes in one Thursday a month) which up to 1997 had last paid a claim in 1923, when Helmut Schmidt's frisky young draft horse kicked in the radiator of Julian Snider's Hupmobile. Schmidt was then declared high-risk and forced into bankruptcy.

When we called the "other company" for a quote, we heard a long soliloquy—something from Wordsworth, I think—then, they informed us that we were, according to industry lingo, "pretty much screwed."

"But why?" I wondered. "We haven't had any claims—none that have been paid anyway—and you have not yet discovered the 17 speeding tickets The Redhead got last month."

It was then explained that they have us over a barrel because we have three vehicles, two of which are SUVs. Insurance companies hate SUVs because the driver of a large SUV is likely to survive an auto accident and therefore is more likely to insist on having the claim paid afterward.

The other problem with owning an SUV is that you have to deal directly with OPEC just to fill your tank, and Venezuela has been testy lately.

According to the "other insurance company," my three vehicles all had high number ratings—25s and 27s—she whispered conspiratorially into the phone. That's bad. Very bad.

I insisted that I should not be charged so much for insurance because although technically I have three vehicles, two of them are stolen, and I'm behind on payments on the other.

That's worse, she said. The cost of insuring my stolen vehicles would bump us to a 29. Maybe even a 30. And even then, the policy would be voided if we actually drove the vehicles.

So we were forced to call our original insurance company on their 400 foot yacht in Barbados, and they said they would take us back if we were nice and promised to send sunscreen right away.

"I don't mind paying more so that you can continue to make outrageous profits," I said. "After all, this is America. But if you have a good year, does that mean we can look forward to a rate reduction?"

She was still laughing when I hung up. I had to hang up because I cannot afford a higher long distance bill.

I already work 112 days a year just to pay my phone bill. Add that to the 116 days I work for the IRS, the 212 days I work for insurance and the 97 days I work to pay for The Redhead's new shoes, and it is clear to me that I must relocate to Mars where the year is 687 days long.

© Tony Bender, 2002

Writer's note: The day this column was published, I was picked up for speeding between Ashley and Wishek. My insurance agent drove by as I was parked with red lights flashing behind me. When I got to my office, a note was waiting for me. "Speeding tickets will cause your premium to rise," my insurance man wrote.

Just another phone company scam

I don't have a problem with a company making a profit. So I'm not one to complain about prices. If I don't like the price, I don't buy it. But some scams you cannot let go unchallenged.

I was just leaving work the other day when one of my employees handed me a long distance phone bill from AT&T for more than $2,000.

We run a small business, and a $2,000 phone bill is definitely out of the ordinary. Now, we had done a project that required many phone calls, but $2,000—that was lots more than I was expecting. I don't usually see the monthly bills, but when something looks amiss, I take a look. We were getting charged about $4 a minute for long distance. Four bucks!

Some time ago, exhausted from all the claims from companies claiming low long distance rates, we decided to just stick with AT&T.

We had tried Sprint. Got ripped. Tried MCI. Don't want to talk about it. So we settled on the name brand, AT&T. I mean, how bad could it be?

It was bad. Two thousand bucks bad. I don't usually conduct business at home, but I was so worked up, I decided to call the AT&T customer service center conveniently located for us prairie dwellers out in Mechanicsburg, Pennsylvania. No answer. So I called in the morning, after tossing and turning and fretting and stewing.

"Hello, AT&T Customer Service. This is Bonnie."

"Hi Bonnie. Are you going to talk dirty to me?"

"I beg your pardon."

"Tell me what you're wearing."

"Sir, this is AT&T!"

"Yeah, I know, but the last time I paid $4 a minute for a phone call, someone talked dirty to me." So tell me, Bonnie, am I making you hot?"

"Sir, if you do not stop this lewd talk, I will have to hang up!"

"OK, let me talk to Miss Cleo, then."

"Miss Who?"

"Gusundhiet!"

"Thank you. Now, who do you wish to speak to?"

"Whom. I think you mean whom. Now, put Miss Cleo on."

"I am not familiar with a Cleo, sir."

"You know, Miss Cleo, the Jamaican soothsayer from

California.

"I'm not following you sir."

"Good. Because that would be stalking. I hope you're not tapping my line, either. But my point is, if I'm going to pay $4 a minute, I ought to get something besides an intra-lata phone call. For that kind of money, Miss Cleo would predict my future. So what do you say? How is this Middle East thing going to sort out?"

"Sir, I have no prediction for you."

"Yeah? Well, I have a prediction for you. I predict I'm not paying this bill! I have a $4.12 charge for a one minute call to Eureka, SD. Do you realize I could drive to Eureka cheaper than that?"

Bonnie forwarded me to another "customer service representative," known to most of you simply as, "Satan."

Satan advised me that according to their records, we were not signed up on any plan with AT&T which allows them to—in layman's terms—"screw you silly."

Almost immediately, though, I was able to negotiate the bill down to 58 cents a minute. I wasn't going for it.

"Look, I see Terry Bradshaw and a gopher advertising a 20 minute phone call for just a buck!"

"You're going to trust a football player over the Devil?"

"No, but I trust the gopher."

Eventually, Old Scratch agreed to adjust the bill to a more moderate 7-14 cents per minute as long as I agreed to one little stipulation, involving, I think, my eternal soul.

I was also invited to sign up for an AT&T business plan involving rates significantly lower than $4 a minute. I decided to study all of our long distance bills and call them back. I discovered that we had been paying $4 a minute for quite some time.

When I called AT&T back, I suggested we ought to adjust all of the bills. However, I was informed that they are not allowed to adjust bills farther back than one month. This comes from the same rule book that allows them to charge $4 a minute. The Devil got kind of testy with me about the whole issue.

Despite the bad attitude, I had decided to go with Satan's business plan. After all, I was grateful at not having a $2,000 bill to pay. But while I was on the line, I was interrupted, so I put the phone on hold for 20 seconds (valued at $1.37.20 by AT&T). When I picked up again, the Devil had hung up.

C'mon! My Aunt Zelda contracted Beri-beri, was hospitalized, eulogized and buried while I was on hold with the phone company one time. And now they couldn't hold for 20 seconds!

So I went with the gopher. But I called my broker this morning. With the money I saved by not getting totally ripped off on the phone bill, I'm investing in AT&T. Those folks are making a killing.

© Tony Bender, 2002

Fear of my meter

At first there were polite messages on the phone. My rural electric company wanted me to read the meter. They have this notion that they need to have these numbers in order to accurately bill me.

Then suspicious-looking unmarked vehicles started driving by slowly. However, it simply may have been townspeople. People around here will make a special effort to drive by your house if you replace the siding. Once, word got out that I had a new riding mower and a string of cars so long crept by, I started looking for the hearse at the head of the line.

But that's the nature of Rural Electric Companies. They are willing to disguise themselves as innocent snoops in order to extract information.

At first I was able to ignore the ever-insistent messages.

Then husky guys in suits and dark sunglasses began showing up at my office cracking their knuckles and speaking sentences completely bereft of the "th" sound.

"We're here to see da boss," dey said. "Tell 'em dis nonsense gotta stop, or he's gonna be typing wit no tums."

"Why would you take away the man's antacid?" Jane asked while I cowered in my office.

"Tums! Tums!" the man barked. "Like on his mitts! We're tum breakers."

"Probably sent by the city council," Jane said after they left. But I know it was the electric company.

Then they got to The Redhead. "Honey, would it really be that hard to walk downstairs and read the meter?" she asked as we snuggled on the couch.

"Arghhh!" I screamed leaping to my feet. "You're one a dem! I mean *them.*"

"Whatever do you mean?" she asked, smiling sweetly.

"You can't fool me, sister! I saw *The Bodysnatchers.* You're wit dem. I mean *with them.*"

She denied it, but I'm keeping an eye on her. I'm walking on pins and needles, here. The other night, she burped at the supper table, and I was convinced an alien was going to burst from her chest and demand a meter reading.

A normal man would have caved in. But not me. The holdout continued.

When we went to Denver for a few days—The Redhead called it a vacation; I was on the lam—the topic came up with friends.

"You mean you actually have to read your own meter?" Bob asked, aghast.

"Yup," I said. "I know if I give in, the phone company is going to expect me to report how many phone calls I'm making each month. This thing could snowball."

Be strong," Bob said, raising his fist to the sky. "Power to the people."

"We shall overcome," I said, weeping.

But when I got back, the pressure began to get unbearable. There were more calls. More letters. "And look," I said, "That car has been past here twice today!"

"That's just the Mehrers," The Redhead said.

"How do we know dey ain't wit dem?" I asked.

"Listen to you," The Redhead chided.

"What? You think I sound paranoid?"

"I think you sound like you're from Brooklyn."

I barricaded myself in the furnace room. A few hours later, I heard Dylan outside the door.

"Mom says it's time to eat."

"Yeah?"

"And she said while you're in there, you should read the meter."

"Et tu, Dylan?" I said.

• • •

Bob called the other day. I dutifully recorded the information for the phone company.

"So you cracked," he said sympathetically.

"Yeah," I said. "They got a whole bunch of people together on the front lawn."

"They smoked you out, huh?"

"Worse. They joined hands and started singing "We Are the World."

"Insidious," he said. "I know how you feel. Once, Rose staged an intervention when I refused to carry out the garbage. They even flew my Mom out from South Dakota. Now, I even have to do the dishes."

"It's hard being a man," I said.

"Hard, indeed," he said.

© Tony Bender, 2002

A lifetime subscription

I don't like to complain... Ahh, who am I kidding? I'm a journalist. I love to complain. And when it's a righteous cause, it really feels good.

Faithful fellow complainers and consumer advocates will remember my widely publicized rants about Sprint, the cable company, Microsoft, all insurance companies and *ESPN, The Magazine.* Of course, since those complaints, they have all ceased business practices I found deceptive and questionable, and are doing a fine job, indeed...

The fact that the ongoing litigation is bankrupting me, and that my lawyer is continuing to duck their calls, has nothing to do with my willingness to say that I like...no, *love* these companies. Of course, I also like the smell of the barnyard in the spring.

Now, get this. I subscribed to *Biography Magazine* for the same reason I subscribe to *TIME* and the *Christian Science Monitor*—because they impress the mailman. But when my subscription ran out, I ignored the increasingly amazing subscription values, including one offering an Hawaiian vacation for two, a BMW, backstage passes for *Barenaked Ladies* (the band) plus $50,000 in cash if I just sent in my $18 *TODAY!*

Biography Magazine, knowing full well that I would be heartbroken if I was unable to experience the monthly joy of scattering throughout my home, like confetti, the 247 cardboard subscription cards they enclose with each issue, decided to resubscribe me. Now that's service. Unfortunately, they still wanted their eighteen bucks.

Then they turned me over to a *pretend* collection agency— The National Credit Audit Corporation, Member of American Collectors Association, Inc. International. Oooooo!

Of course, the COLLECTION NOTICE was appropriately covered with intimidating red ink.

"The publisher has turned your account over to us for collection. All communication should be with National Credit Audit Corporation... Thank you for your prompt cooperation so that further collection activity on our part can be avoided."

The threat went on in legalese demanding "pursuant to the "Fair Debt Collection Practices Act" that we call *LONG DISTANCE* (because they are in cahoots with my long distance carrier) to explain exactly why we were not willing to commit to a lifetime subscription of *Biography Magazine*. The letter was signed by

Seymour Cardoza of the Peoria, Ill, Cardozas.

I looked up the NCAC on the Internet and the first thing I found was a class action suit filed against them by the Chicago law firm of *Edelman, Combs & Latturner*, for violations of the Fair Debt Collection Practices Act, specifically for their subscription renewal collection tactics. They were probably framed.

Unbeknownst to me, The Redhead called NCAC, confident that I must be guilty of *something*. She heard a recording of her Miranda rights and then was assured by Mongo, a customer service hit man, that there would be no jail time for her if she rolled over on me. In the interest of the children, she did.

As a newspaper owner, I am a professional when it comes to dealing with subscriptions—or prescriptions, as they refer to them around here, because we alternately have the ability to heal with our sage words or leave you snoozing in boredom like a good muscle relaxant.

I'm old school. I know the way things should work when a subscription expires. We send out the notice—sans red ink—and then the customer comes to our front desk and threatens *us*. Because there's never anything in the newspaper. And we're unreasonably expensive. Then they subscribe anyway.

I fully intend to give Seymour a piece of my mind. I might call collect. After all they are a collection agency. Or I will list my grievances in a voluminous letter. Then I will rub it in the dark, musky recesses of my arm pit after not bathing for a week and mail it—postage due.

© Tony Bender, 2002

You say yer uh nus,
I say yer anus

Oh, no. You don't get off that easy. You teachers aren't going to sneak this one past Old Tone. Couldn't handle the pressure, could you? Couldn't handle a few jokes. So you had to change the rules.

I'm talking about something of cosmic proportions here. The third biggest planet. The seventh from the sun. I'm talking about Uranus.

When Dylan was sharing what he had learned in school recently, he rattled off the names of the planets. You got Saturn, Venus, Mars and Uranus. *Yer uh' nus* he pronounced it.

What?! Where did that "uh" sound come from? Everyone knows it's pronounced *yer anus*. It's been pronounced that way since Uranus was invented back in 1492.

C'mon now. It's even spelled Ur *anus!* How can you deny mil-

lions of school children the chance to chortle during astronomy?
A kid gets one laugh during a semester of dreary talk about
black holes and quasars and quarks and now our educational
system has taken it away.

Why in my day, we loved learning about the planets.

"Hey, Miss Simpkins?"

"Yes, Tony?"

"Have you ever seen yer anus?"

(Yuk, yuk.)

"Of course I have, Tony."

"Hey, is it true there are rings around Yer anus?" (Hysterical
laughter in the classroom. Leroy falls out of his chair.)

"As a matter of fact, Tony, scientists have recently discovered
rings. It is believed that the greenish hue of the planet is due to
a concentration of methane gas."

"So I guess yer anus stinks!" (More laughter, and I get sent to
the office.)

Nowadays, kids probably have never seen the inside of the
principal's office (or orifice as we called it in my day when anything butt-related was hilarious).

Why in third grade Mrs Bloomer stuffed herself into a girdle
so tight, if it ever burst, all 37 of us would have been killed by
Playtex shrapnel. One day, unbeknownst to her, she split a seam
down the back of her dress. For the same reason no one ever
tells you when you are walking around with your fly open, we
failed to advise her of her predicament. But when she had a
coughing fit, Hawkeye became convinced the girdle was gonna

blow.

"Duck and cover!" he screamed as we evacuated.

"What's going on!" Mr. Hanson, the fifth grade teacher, asked as we scurried down the stairs.

"B-bbig hole," I stuttered with his hand on my shoulder.

"Where?" he asked, alarmed.

"Yer anus!" I said. (Ricky Head blows snot out of his ears from laughing. I am sent to the office.)

I guarantee you this pronunciation change is no coincidence. Name one other planet that has changed its pronunciation.

Venus is still *vee nus*. It rhymes with anus. However, if you changed the pronunciation to be consistent with the new pronunciation of Uranus, you would pronounce Venus as *Venice*.

And Pluto would be *pluh toe* if we were going to follow that logic.

Don't even try to tell me there isn't some sort of conspiracy here. You know darn well they flew a bunch of teachers (who can't take a joke) to a secret location in black helicopters to discuss the change with our shadow government.

"OK, boys, we've hoaxed a moon landing, turned the populace into zombies with fluoride in the water and paid the CIA for killing Kennedy. What else is on the agenda?"

"Yer anus!" a voice pipes up. (Dick Cheney squirts coffee out of his nostrils.)

"Pardon?" the chairman says.

"Uranus, sir," a science teacher from Duluth responds. "We need to change the pronunciation to *yer uh nus* because school children are having too much fun with the old pronunciation."

"Well, we can't have that," the chairman says. "Done. Now let's get back to this one world government thing... Elvis, what do you think?"

And another thing. I've about had it with Martha Stewart. I'm not all that worked up about the insider trading and the whole rich get richer while the rest of us starve thing. I'm OK with that. It's Wall Street. It's the American way.

No, what has me upset is her pronunciation of herb. I personally remember being heckled for pronouncing it just like it is spelled. Herb. Like Herb Tarlick, the salesman from WKRP. But then, everyone got all hoity-toity on us and decided to drop the "h" sound. Fine. I dealt with it. Urb it is.

But now, Martha Stewart has taken it upon herself to start calling urbs herbs (with the h sound) again just because she has the power.

But if everyone starts changing pronunciations willy-nilly, it'll be anarchy! Did anyone clear this with Elvis?

That's why Martha Stewart must be imprisoned (in a room with delicate pastels and fresh cut daisies). Hey Martha, get your head out of Uranus! (Yuk.)

© Tony Bender, 2002

FRIENDS INDEED

The turn
taken

I would drive south past the exit. I would drive north on I-29, seeing the sign every time. Back and forth. Up and down. I passed the exit 100 times.

It was 6:30 last Saturday night, and I was headed for Watertown and a night alone in another motel room.

I passed the time and the miles fantasizing about the supper I would have. There had been two over-ripe bananas for breakfast at another motel and a big golden delicious apple for lunch—not nearly enough—and had decided I would find the best restaurant in town, no matter what the cost, and that is where I would eat. A lot.

I had seen the sign in the morning, and like always, I was too busy to pull over, but I sent fond thoughts floating into Castlewood, where they would be felt, I am sure, and perhaps, provide a little warmth even as I sped past through the remains of the first winter storm.

Now, as I was coming back north, my empty stomach demanded I press on. But this time when I saw the sign, I slowed and pulled to the right, confounding my schedule and my stomach. Another left and eight miles of curvy winter blacktop would get me there. I thought about calling ahead, but soon enough he would know I was coming.

Eight short miles. I had not known it was that close. Sometimes, especially in December, the burgs seems so far apart in South Dakota. Each sign off the Interstate heralds a town to the right or to the left, and after you've lived out here for a while, you start to know that the spaces between where you are and where you want to be are generally quite a stretch.

But this was eight miles. Eight minutes. I thought about the times I had driven past. One soul sliding past on the four lane marvel, another soul, an old friend, parked in a recliner, silent except for the chatter of the television and the jingle of the dog's collar as he stretches or scratches.

That's where he was when I pulled into the driveway behind his car. Through the window, I could see him rise and walk to the door.

It had not been hard to find his home though the kid behind the counter at the gas station had not known the location nor had the woman renting the video. How can you live in a small town and not know where everyone lives? I wondered. Especially a guy like Carl. I knew he was special. How could you live in the same town and not know?

But I suppose it is the distance of generations, the modesty of one, the indifference of the other, that is the explanation.

It had been twenty years, and he had not changed and even in his eighties, his face was remarkably unlined. But I had changed. In the mirror, I see the skin beginning to sag, the lines furrowing deep. He did not recognize me.

Still, he was opening his home to me all the while he was listening to my introduction.

Notre Dame was leading Purdue, and I saw Carl's gaze return to the screen a few times the way mine does when I have to split my attention between visitors and the Vikings.

I explained to Carl why I had decided to stop and he said he understood. He, too, drives by exits and old friends.

"I always think there's not enough time," he said. "But there's not any more time the next time."

I nodded. It just didn't seem right, all this driving by, all these years. This is where my friend Bob had grown up and though he had been to my family home in Frederick many times, I had never been to his.

"I thought I should see where Bob came from," I told Carl. Us being best friends and all.

Carl showed me Bob's old room upstairs. It was bright blue, and the walls angled in to accommodate the pitch of the roof a lot like my old pale blue room.

I saw the old pictures in black and white of Bob and his brothers. Gary was 15 when they lost him to leukemia, Carl told me impassively, but I knew it was still hard. I did the math. Bob must have been about five at the time.

And then there was Don who was the middle child and then the oldest, and Bob's twin, a girl, who was dead at birth.

So this is where my friend had come from. A home a lot like mine had been. I felt like I was intruding, spying even, but we are good enough friends, I know, so he will not mind, and he will be pleased I took the time to stop.

"So how are you doing, Carl?" I asked.

"Good. I'm doing good. But my wife is in the nursing home, and that's not good."

"I know," I said.

I stayed about 45 minutes, and I let him know just how important his son was to me, how he had stood by me in good times and bad.

"As you go on in this life," I said, "You start to realize how few and far between loyal, true friends are."

Carl was proud of Bob, I could see, as we compared notes about the son and the friend 700 miles away in Denver. Carl was back in his chair, a Bible visible under the newspaper on the table to the left. Seventies shag carpet separated us from the muted television.

When I started repeating myself, and I had run out of things to say, I rose to leave. Carl yelped a bit at a Notre Dame interception then turned his attention back to me. He walked me to the door, and the dog did not fuss quite so much this time.

"Give Phyllis a hug for me. Tell her hello," I said as I opened

58

the vehicle door. Carl said that he would.

I could see him standing in the door as I backed out, watching as I drove away.

Forty-five minutes later, I was in a poorly-lit booth where the transplanted southern waitress called me "Hon."

I scanned the menu.

I wasn't quite so hungry now.

© Tony Bender, 2001

Things
gained

He had tea—some exotic concoction perfect for a November morning had it not been nearly tropical outside, short-sleeve weather. He was wearing shorts, blue jean cutoffs, when he opened the door to let me in. Excellent attire for the gift of the day, as the sun steamed away traces of South Dakota fog.

The conversation was easy, and he wondered if I remembered the song dancing across the speakers. I listened and at first I could not get it, but when I closed my eyes it came to me. "Ambrosia," I said. *"Time Waits For No One."* He smiled beneath the gray beard because I had passed the test. His eyes laughed like they always had, warm and youthful still. We talked about decades past, my trails and trials and his, of joys past and sorrows heavy. There had been so many losses, I said, not mourning, not complaining, just matter of fact. He nodded, his silver ponytail bobbing on his back, looking for all the world like Santa in the Sixties, "Ah," he smiled kindly, "But to have lost something, you must have first gained something."

• • •

I was in the bookstore a few hours later when I saw her, separated from me by the volumes and tomes of wisdom and folly and all else the publishers deem worthy of our contemplations.

I stood beside my mother and waved, and though she was only visible from the nose on up, I know she smiled because I saw her eyes join in the greeting. I moved two steps forward, and she stepped from behind the books, and we smiled some more at each other. She was with her mother, too.

"Come," I said, eager like a child to show parents a marvelous new toy in the shop window. "I want you to meet my mother."

"This is someone very important," I told my mother, as if she could not see by my actions that she was. "This is the lady who delivered India...Dr. Born."

We had come to her, Julie and I, at a time when uncertainty felt like a comfort, when grievous losses seemed to loom around every corner, ready to pounce. As we had sought to grow our family beyond three, there had been losses. Terrible, unfathomable losses. In that examination room, Dr. Born nodded as we told the story, though she knew it already from the clinical

61

descriptions of the file. She could not tell us that this time every-thing would be fine because there are no guarantees in this life, except maybe that there will be twists unforeseen and turns unimagined. But she comforted, she soothed with her manner and though she did not say it, we came to believe that things would work out after all, this time. We sensed her resolve to do what she could for us and for little India, then unborn, who now smiles and coos and hugs and cuddles us and gives us joys worth waiting for.

Introductions complete, her mother said to mine about me, "He is such a nice man!" In anguish, I turned to my mother, standing behind me like a manager in a prize fight, because I know it is not the truth. My mother, who has witnessed deeds and thoughts so dark, looked me in the eye and then, brown eyes twinkling, turned to them and silently drew her hand across her mouth, zipping it shut. There we stood, smiling, grin-ning at each other, the doctor and me, our mothers in our cor-ners, both beaming and proud. But when we met in the middle of the ring, we hugged. And then she went to seek a chiropractic cure.

• • •

I was driving through the North Dakota Badlands the next morning, contemplating the forces that had drawn old friends together, smiling and seeming to know, somewhere in the back of our minds, deep in the recesses of our souls, some wonderful secret. A secret we could feel but not really express.

The fog was thick and only the road was visible, but the guardrails to the right told me of the dangers below. Around one curve the fog suddenly was gone, repelled by some invisible barrier, and I could see the majesty I had been missing, a spectacular, rugged timescape, another planet almost.

I smiled at the beauty, at the surprise. Even though I had driven this road before and knew what was there, when it appeared, it caused me to exalt and to applaud the handiwork of the wind, the rain, the eons and God.

• • •

That is how the Tiny Dancer, The Poet, had appeared the day before, the day after Thanksgiving, suddenly, as if there was a break in the weather. "The Great and Mighty Da-Da!" she announced, laughing, I think, at the thought of the changes in my life since we met more than 20 years ago.

"An old flame," I explained to another friend standing beside me, who excused herself to give us time.

"You said you were going to be famous," the Tiny Dancer said. (She thinks I am.)

"I said that?!" I blustered, flustered, unable to imagine that audacity. It's funny. I look back, and I do not remember myself. I know where I have been, but somehow I can only remember little snippets of who I was, what I was and what I was feeling then. Maybe it's just as well.

"You insisted!" she laughed, her grin a little crooked, her eyes scrunching up mischievously just like they always did.

"I've been reading about The Redhead," she said, smiling some more. "She's great!" she said, pumping her fist in solidarity.

"Yes, she is," I said, leaning back, comfortable, basking in my good fortune. Though it does not seem possible, her crooked grin widens. She apologizes for not seeing me before, when there were opportunities, and she explains. "I never looked right. And you always said I was pretty. I never felt I looked pretty enough. But this time I said, 'I'm going no matter how I look!'" Did it bother me that she had avoided me before, she wondered? "No," I said. "I always knew I was in good standing with you."

• • •

I was about to leave when Nancy glided in, serious, on a mission. She is the wise one, a friend to Julie and me.

"Come sit awhile," I said, knowing one must take time for the moments the cosmos so brilliantly arranges on days like these.

She asked about Julie, and I smiled the distant smile I always do as I try to picture her in my mind as I speak about her. "And the kids are doing great, too," I continued.

"Make sure you teach Dylan about spirituality," Nancy, our angel, insists. I tell her of the steps we have taken as she nods in approval, her eyes searching mine to see if I am telling the truth. "I'm not worried about him," I say. "He has a good heart.

He has his mother's heart." Nancy listens to me, and she is sat-isfied that quality parenting is taking place. Otherwise she would call us in and give us a good talking to as she has done before.

"And you, Nancy," I ask. "How are you? How are your eyes?" When I saw her last, she was losing her vision, and she was frightened I could see. But the surgeons had fixed her eyes, she told me. Now she could see the skip in the child's gait, laces undone, dragging through the dust. Now she could see the lines in the faces in the lines at the stores.

I had already guessed the answer. She looked younger, serene again. She sees clearly again. And I see so much more clearly today than I did yesterday.

• • •

As I drove the Badlands, remembering the gift of yesterday, I spotted a hulking dark brown dog, trotting purposefully toward me in the ditch on the opposite side of the road.

He has a bulldog face, the body of something else and bul-let-black eyes. And he looked at me and I at him as he trotted, miles from any home, down the rise. His face seemed to have a jowly sort of smile, and it made the corners of my mouth edge upward in mirth.

I saw him in the mirror as I rounded the curve, never break-ing stride. He seemed to know where he is going.

© Tony Bender, 2001

65

Old friends
of the heart

I keep them in my heart. That's where I keep my old friends.

We thought our gang was special back in high school—that our friendships would endure. Most of them have. Some evaporated, and the last I saw of them was a gold tassel dangling at graduation, marching resolutely away.

There were nearly 50 of us in the Class of '76. I'm sure it was the largest graduation class ever in that town of 400. But our gang extended a few grades up and a few down. We cherry-picked the best and the brightest, the funniest and the most loyal, and then we spent weekends parked in pastures laughing.

The gang was malleable. There were those who floated in and floated out, but once a member always a member.

At our 10 year class reunion, the gang was the same, but in the rest of the class, some wallflowers had bloomed spectacularly.

I missed the next reunion. I don't know why. Can't explain it. I wasn't living far away. I must have been immersed in some sort of funk. "You should have been there," they said. Yeah. Yeah, I should have been there.

The thing is, keeping friends in your heart is fine and all. It's the best you can do most of the time. But when you get the chance to take them out and play with them, you must.

I couldn't wait for last weekend to get here. Couldn't wait to see who would come out to play at the all-school reunion. It's been 26 years. Wow. I just saw the words "26 years" on the screen and now I am somewhat stunned. Back then, when we talked about being friends for life, I don't think we ever imagined we would get here, 26 years into the future. I never imagined my friends being grandparents. But it's happening.

A few weeks ago, I mentioned the "amazing Annie Oschner" in a column. I was unloading my car, having just pulled into town, when three people stopped on the street in front of me.

"Tony? Is that you?"

"Help me," I said, trying to see past the beard, the sunglasses and the years. It was Mark Oschner and his wife. "And you know who this is, don't you?"

I panicked. Who was that behind those sunglasses? It was the Amazing Annie Oschner.

"Annie's in town," I told a friend that night.

"Annie Oschner?"

"Yes," I said. "And she still has that wicked little smile and that wicked little laugh." And in that moment, I had defined exactly what it was I had found amazing about Annie three decades and more back.

And Donna was back from Hollywood. I spotted her through the crowd, and even from the back I knew it was her. I dragged The Redhead over to meet my very first junior high girlfriend.

I had given her a three dollar ring I bought from Norm Glarum at the drug store. Donna told The Redhead that she had worn it on a chain around her neck because it was too big for her long, slender fingers. I, however, remember her wrapping yarn around it, in the custom of the day, so it would fit. Now, I am not sure whose memory is correct.

She laughed her big joyous laugh, her head flying back to let out the sounds, when she confessed she was afraid that she would get pregnant if we held hands on the fan bus. She remembered us kissing, but I know she is wrong about that. Not that I didn't try. We did hold hands though. And she did not get pregnant.

The conversation moved to makeup—*I know I didn't bring it up*—and Donna said she never wears makeup. Certainly, she is the only one in southern California.

Then she told us why. For one thing, she doesn't have to. Her skin remains tan and flawless. But once, she put on a bit of makeup and me, being a Neanderthal, told her it made her look like a hooker.

I don't remember saying such a thing. And I don't recall having much experience with hookers, either, back in seventh grade, but clearly I scarred her. I feel kind of bad about it. On the other hand, I can't believe anyone could take what a seventh grader says seriously.

She kissed me goodnight when she left, thereby settling the issue of whether we had ever kissed. She kissed The Redhead, too, on the lips, because it's a Hollywood thing. Donna works in a production company for Bill Murray. "Bill," she called him.

Mary was there and Woof and Whitey. My hair was perfectly coiffed in the bedhead look, but Whitey took one look at the unruly clumps sticking up and dubbed me Kicking Bird (as in Dances with Wolves). He spent the rest of the night talking to me in Lakota.

"Tatanka," he said.

"Shut up," I said.

As I defended myself from the ribbing, I realized that Whitey and Woof were, and always have been, funnier than me. If they ever start a newspaper column, I am screwed.

A goateed face under a big white cowboy hat peered down at me while I was sitting. I didn't figure it out at first, but when the first syllable drawled out of his mouth, I got up and gave him a hug. "Muck!" He's in Texas now. He hates it there.

But Witte wasn't there. Or Katie, and she only lives 26 miles away. And Leroy. I haven't seen him for 20 years. Not since he disappeared into the Air Force and got all serious and somber. Rietta stayed in Nebraska.

But Al Cat was there. And Jay Bird. Hawkeye, too. And Gare Bare. I already have my pictures back, and he and I are sitting in front of the Northern Lights Lounge at 2:30 a.m., red-faced and winding down. I remember heckling my younger brother as he walked home a few minutes earlier. "You gonna let us old-timers outlast you?"

He was.

Under the circumstances, I think we look pretty good. Gare has less hair. I'm jowly, and my forehead has grown. But Annie still has that wicked little smile, and Donna still looks terrific even without makeup.

I'm a little worried about the kiss, though. I hope she doesn't get pregnant.

© Tony Bender, 2002

Editor's note: Leroy e-mailed me after he got wind of the column, complaining about being depicted as serious and somber. He was serious and somber the last time I saw him, I replied. "In fact, I think you were singing dirges."

Hunter
Joe

I was juggling luggage as I struggled to lock the door to my third-floor dorm room at SDSU. Easter vacation—a chance to fire up the old Grey Ghost and head for home.

On my way out, in the nearly-deserted hall, I ran into Philly Joe. For the want of a plane ticket, Joe was going to spend Easter vacation alone in the dorm.

"Get your stuff," I ordered. I knew full well that I wasn't going to enjoy my vacation with the thought of Joe, alone in the dorm. And if Mom found out I'd left him there, she'd make me turn around and get him. Not that she knew Joe. That's just the way all Moms are.

So, that's really how it all started—how Philly Joe became Hunter Joe. I don't remember exactly how Joe and I became friends. We were an odd couple. He was a good student. I was a stranger to my instructors.

Joe had been sent to school by his parents to keep him off the streets. I'd gone to Moo U, not because I had any overwhelming desire to continue my education, but because I was darn sure I wasn't ready to join the work force.

It was an early spring, moist, warm and green, and along the way home we saw hordes of gophers. "When we get home, we're going gopher hunting," I told Joe. He was all for it.

Saturday found us in Orville Crawford's yard asking for permission. Orville explained that the big black and white things were cows, but anything else out there was fair game. Orville thinks he's pretty funny—sort of a Henny Youngman of the plains.

We had Grandpa Ben's single shot .22, and that gun has seen some good shooters in its time. I used to be a fair shot, but my Mom was the Grim Reaper of Gophers.

Grandpa developed a healthy respect for Mom's marksmanship the day she dropped 21 out of 22 gophers—21 in a row. The first shot sailed over the critter's head because Grandpa forgot to tell her the rifle "shoots a little high." After that, gophers fell like dominoes. After each direct hit, Grandpa would slap his overall-clad knee and exclaim, "Golly!" This was the proud history of the Coast to Coast brand .22 single-shot, bolt-action rifle.

Well, I knocked down a few gophers, missed a few more and Joe did the same. The sun was threatening to set when Joe spotted something running nearly a quarter mile away—a big old jackrabbit. Since it wasn't a cow, Joe wanted to shoot it.

I explained to Joe that the rabbit was clearly out of reasonable range, it was on the run, and besides, the wind was still swirling around as it does most days on the prairie.

Still, Joe wanted to try. It seemed like an eternity from the time Joe fired to the time the bullet arrived. I watched the jackrabbit loping, threatening to clear the crest of the hill.

That's as far as he got.

I couldn't help myself. I slapped my knee and in spite of myself, uttered the first and last "golly" of my life. It seemed to me that Joe stood a little taller at that moment.

Now, I've seen photos of hunters with some mighty impressive trophies, but I've never seen a prouder hunter than Joe. It was all I could do to convince him that we couldn't eat it. But I relented when he insisted we bring the prize home for a photo session.

Somewhere, in some shoebox, I've got that photo of Hunter Joe, holding that big old jack in the early stages of rigor mortis, stretching nearly the length of Joe's 5-6 body.

Later, I inspected the rabbit from end to end, but I never did find a bullet hole. Though I never told Joe, I always believed that the lead fell from the sky just hard enough to knock the poor beast dead. Or maybe that old rabbit just picked that moment to drop dead of a heart attack.

But that will have to be our secret.

Because someday, somewhere in Philadelphia, Joe will have a wide-eyed grandchild on his knee, and he'll tell him about The Greatest Shot.

Joe's eyes will sparkle and he'll laugh.

Maybe he'll even slap his knee and say "golly."

Why would we want to ruin a moment like that?

© Tony Bender, 1995

✍ PRAIRIE BEAT

Lady sings the blues again

I never got it. Never understood The Redhead's infatuation with Billie Holiday. Still, I enabled her. I bought her CDs when I found them in the jazz section. I even surrendered a precious slot on my 1973 Seeburg Matador jukebox for *"God Bless the Child."*

But understand? Never did. I would listen to the crackly old recordings, and I would know she was good. But special? I was not convinced.

Billie Holiday and Ella Fitzgerald were contemporaries in the Thirties, Forties and Fifties, and Ella's longevity is what helped capture me. She endured long enough for recording technologies to muster enough fidelity to capture the greatness to tape.

Billie Holiday's greatest sin was not the booze and the drugs which prematurely ended the song at 43 in 1959. It was that she arrived too early to be recorded decently.

So I never understood The Redhead's love for Billie Holiday. Could not grasp the depths of admiration expressed by the old jazz men of the era. I find myself listening to the later recordings of Sinatra, Torme, Bennett, Ella and Louie because of my prejudice against those faded old recordings.

But I've tried listening. I've tried.

So I settle for the the older singer, when voices are not as strong or supple, but experience and guile, I think, make them great. And sometimes greater.

I bought the 1958 recording of *Lady in Satin*, Billie Holiday's last, recorded 17 months before her death. I hoped I would hear greatness. The Redhead slid the gleaming CD into the slot as we cruised North Dakota two lanes in the Mustang.

This time the crackles and scratches were not on the tape, but in her voice. We both cringed. Even I knew, her voice on this last recording was barely a hint of what it had been.

How could this have been, as legend has it, Billie Holiday's favorite album? How could otherwise sage trumpet player Buck Clayton have believed the later Billie Holiday was the greater?

The arrangements by Ray Ellis and his forty-two piece orchestra, were lush, providing a grand stage for a voice to frolic. When I dragged my step-dad Jim, an old jazz drummer, downstairs for a listen, he nodded. "A good arranger could make *me* sound good," he said. But Jim is not a singer.

Billie had heard the young Ellis' work and knew if there was anything left inside her, he could bring it out. And when they heard Lady would record again, musicians scrambled to become part of the project.

She was nervous when she walked into the studio that last time. But the musicians applauded and seemed to soothe her. She was still a diva. Still carried with her the demons. They discovered pure gin in her water pitcher. Life had taken a steep toll.

"When I heard the first playback, I was quite shook up," Ellis remembered. "The quality of Billie's voice had really deteriorated." It was not until later, Ellis admits, that he grasped the greatness of her recording.

The musicians must have known at the moment. "The reaction was quite fascinating," Ellis says. "They crowded into the control room after each good take."

The Redhead was disappointed. I could see it as we listened. But I kept listening. I played it when I drove. It plays on my stereo at 6 a.m. this morning as I write. Even when the music has stopped, I can hear the plaintive voice on *The End of a Love Affair.*

So I walk a little too fast,
And I drive a little too fast,
And I'm reckless, it's true,
But what else can you do at the end of a love affair?
So I talk a little too much,
And I laugh a little too much,
And my voice is a little too loud,
When I'm out in a crowd,

So that people are apt to stare... *

"I found myself watching her reactions as she was hearing each arrangement for the first time," Ellis writes in the liner notes. "When the strings ascended or ended in a tremolo, she would turn to me and smile. The most emotional moment was her listening to the playback of *I'm a Fool to Want You.* There were tears in her eyes."

As I have savored each note, I finally hear what I could not before. I hear Billie Holiday's heart And though she died when I was just six months old, I miss her. The Redhead has been patient with my new infatuation because, after all, it was she who introduced us.

But she doesn't get it.

At long last, though, I do.

© Tony Bender, 2001

* Edward C. Redding

He never
cheated da notes

I called Booker the next day. He'd understand. The Man was gone. Can't pretend it's just another day.

"Yeah, Frank cashed 'em," Booker said irreverently from his kitchen in Denver. No sense being maudlin.

I don't know how many times we'd belted out Sinatra songs while spinning records for weddings and dances.

We were both working for KHOW in Denver in the early 80s and we played a lot of Sinatra. I have to smile thinking back... A couple of long-haired disc jockeys cranking up the sound in the studio and singing along at the top of our lungs.

That's life,
That's what all the people say,

81

You're riding high in April,
Shot down in May... *

"I remember belting out that song walking across the parking lot at the mall," Booker said. "People were looking at us."

The song and the singer had an impact. That's Life. That's how my newspaper column got its name.

I've been a puppet, a pauper, a pirate,
a poet, a pawn and a king.
I've been up and down and over and out
and I know one thing,
Each time I find myself flat on my face,
I pick myself up and get back in the race. *

Tony Bennett, who Sinatra said was his favorite singer, contemplated a world without Sinatra. "I'm reminded of the day Gershwin died," Bennett said. "One of his best friends was told about it, and he just stared. 'Gershwin died,' he said. 'Gershwin died?' "And then he said, 'I don't have to believe that.'"

The music lives on.

A million critics have tried to describe what made Sinatra great. For me, it was the way he phrased a song. In *I Like to Lead When I Dance,* he incorporates a stutter.

There's only one problem,
The t-t-tiniest problem

82

✍ PRAIRIE BEAT

*I like to lead when I dance...***

Perfect imperfection. Sinatra was a perfectionist, a wrong note, unforgivable. In an out-take on *How Little We Know*, Frank calls a halt to the music, a little disgusted with himself. "I'm just trying to cheat da notes," he says. "You can't cheat da notes. Ya gotta sing 'em." He was hard on himself in other ways, too. Before an appearance, his voice ravaged by the nightlife, he chided himself. "Drink, drink, drink. Smoke, smoke, smoke. Schmuck, schmuck, schmuck."

I loved his style, his braggadocio. In the sixties when he and Count Basie were playing the Sands, after the introduction, Ol' Blue Eyes steps up to the mike and intones, "How'd all these people get in my room?" A line swiped from Dean Martin. Then he breaks into *Come Fly With Me*.

So cool.

In 1993, when Sinatra recorded *Duets*, it was panned by some critics. It ticked me off a bit. Here's a guy in his late seventies, still cranking it out... Give the guy a break. His voice wasn't the same—but it was still a marvelous instrument—guile and style substituting for youth. He was older but still defiant. Still cheeky. When he and aging Charles Aznavour sing *You Make me Feel so Young*, you have to grin. There's no stopping it.

You make me feel so young,
You make me feel spring has sprung,
Every time I see you grin,

83

*I'm such a koo-koo individual...****

Frank Sinatra never stopped being cool. And he never, never, cheated the notes.

© Tony Bender, 1998

* Dean Kay-Kelly Gordon, recorded 11/21/61

** Sammy Cahn-Jimmy Van Heusen, recorded 4/8/64

***Josef Myrow-Mack Gordon, recorded 6/6/93

Bobby, Tommy
Dee and me

Charlie Fox gave me the assignment and the phone numbers. Call 'em, he said. Tape the interviews, and we'll play them on the air.

"On the air" was KQDJ-Jamestown. It was my first full time radio job, and I was being paid $700 a month, and now I would interview the stars.

I'd seen Tommy Roe on television on some corny Saturday afternoon rock and roll show when *Dizzy* was big and my favorite song. And when the announcer joked with the singer, calling him Tommy Row Boat, I thought it was just about the cleverest thing I had ever heard emanating from the same black and white Zenith TV that would spew the drama of another edited Notre Dame loss on Sunday morning.

Now I had Tommy Roe's phone number. And Dee Clark's.

Clark had that big hit with *Raindrops* in 1961 when I was three. But it still popped up in oldies rotation enough, so if you had heard of rock and roll, you had heard of Dee Clark or at least knew the words to *Raindrops*.

Bobby Vee, who was headlining the upcoming concert in Jamestown, had sent Charlie a copy of Dee Clark's Greatest Hits from his very own record collection. I remember holding the album, my hands touching the very same record that had been tucked away on a shelf in Bobby Vee's home.

Bobby was patient as we worked through the interview, repeating the story of the day the music died and Buddy Holly's plane ended up in an Iowa corn field and he missed the gig in Moorhead in 1959 and every one thereafter.

Waylon Jennings, one of the new Crickets, had kidded Holly before the plane took off, "I hope your ole' plane crashes." Jennings sang *Donna* that night in Moorhead for the very young and very dead Richie Valens.

Fifteen-year-old Bobby Vee and the Shadows were among the local talent hired to fill the unfillable void.

Once we got past the obligatory Buddy Holly connection, I was delighted to learn that one Robert Zimmerman had played with Bobby Vee in 1959, and Bobby was delighted to tell the story. The band decided they needed a piano player, but that was before keyboards were portable, and the plan died early. The first gig with Zimmerman, who called himself Elston Gunnn (with three n's), was in Gwinner.

A few years later, Bobby Vee was on the East Coast to see the newest folk legend, this guy they'd all been hearing about—Bob Dylan.

When the wiry, curly-headed singer took the stage, Bobby Vee whispered to a friend, "Hey, that's Zimmerman!"

Tommy Roe was a good interview, too, polite enough when the conversation veered from *Sweet Pea, Hooray for Hazel, Jam Up and Jelly Tight,* and *Sheila,* to tell me about his touring days with the Beatles, when Tommy was the headliner and the Fab Four stole the show.

There were fist fights between John and Paul on the bus, he said. They really went at it, Tommy said.

The night of the show in Jamestown, I sat backstage with Tommy and Dee. Bobby must have been on first.

They talked about the business. The ups. The downs. The time Tommy was robbed in his hotel room at gunpoint and how he could have been a dead man but just lost a lot of jewelry.

I wondered aloud, somewhere in the conversation, where Jim Croce would have gone if his plane hadn't crashed in '72. Far, said Dee. "He was in the pocket!" Tommy nodded.

When it was time for Tommy to go on, he tried to talk me into going on stage instead. "C'mon, it'll be fun," he said. But I didn't have the guts. I stayed backstage with Dee.

I had taken a shine to Dee, and I'd like to think that he liked me, too. When we had talked on the phone, I could tell he was pleased that I had done my homework. I'd listened to the music. *Just Keep it Up. Hey, Little Girl. How About That* and *Raindrops.* But my favorite song was *Portrait of my Love.*

When I guessed that Dee had emulated Nat King Cole on the song, Dee was pleased, and I could feel him smiling through the phone line from Atlanta. Yes, he said. That was one of his favorites, too. And yes, he was emulating the great Nat King Cole.

Dee's voice was clear and resonant that night. Powerful. If he had lost anything in 20 years, I could not hear it.

After singing the hits and knocking them dead, he resurrected a ballad that never went far for him on the charts, so I don't suppose he sang it much.

"This one is for a friend of mine, Tony," he said, as I watched from backstage.

Anyone who sees her,
soon forgets the Mona Lisa!
It would take I know,
a Michael Angelo,
and he would need
the glow of dawn
that paints the sky above
to try an' paint a portrait of my love!*

He sang beautifully.

Tommy Roe sent lots of records after that night, and I played them for awhile; even though, they never became hits. Because it wouldn't have seemed right not to, us being friends and all.

I kept their phone numbers, and I'm sure they're still in my Rolodex under M for memories. I called Bobby once after Charlie Fox left the radio station. I left a message wondering how I could return the Dee Clark record. But Bobby never called back.

Dee Clark died in 1990, seven or eight years after the concert. Heart attack. He was 52 and no longer in the pocket. So now if Bobby ever calls, I'm not taking the call, and I'm keeping the record.

© Tony Bender, 2002

* Music by Cyril Ornadel
with lyrics by David West, 1961

Voices on
the radio

The voices spoke to me through the radio. Big voices.
Amiable voices. Important voices.

They boomed through the lone, tinny speaker of the transistor radio I got for my birthday. Or for Christmas. I don't remember which, but the important thing is I had it.

I burned through nine volt batteries the way chain smokers burned through cigarettes at the bar on Saturday night.

In my room (OK, so I shared it with three younger brothers, but it was still *my* room.) with Peter Max posters asserting my rock 'n roll identity, the voices were the last thing I heard as drifted off in the summer evenings in the two-story Leesburg house my parents rented for $60 a month. If my mother did not tip-toe in and click off the radio at midnight, the voices faded by morning, and another battery was shot.

I mowed lawns and shoveled sidewalks and delivered newspapers and sold garden seeds and Christmas cards to support my battery purchases and a serious pinball addiction.

I fed the ravenous jukebox in the City Cafe quarters, playing the Cufflinks's *Tracy* over and over again, a measure of my passionate and unspoken seventh grade crush on Tracy Lahr who was much older—*in eighth grade!*—and had the most charmingly prominent nose, attractive in a gangly Sarah Jessica Parker sort of way. In fact, she invented Sarah Jessica Parker.

"*Bah, bah bah bah bah bah,*" the lyrics went, and they reached me.

Tracy, when I'm with you
Somethin' you do bounces me off the ceiling
Tracy, day after day
When you're this way, I get a lovin' feelin'

Come with me, don't say "No"
Hold me close, Tracy never let me go

Tracy, you're gonna be
Happy with me, I'll build a world around you
Filled with love everywhere
*And when you're there you'll be so glad I found you**

Of course, it didn't work out that way. Tracy never knew

about my crush, and when she reads this it will be a revelation for her. She must have thought it was mere coincidence that the song played every time she and I were in the cafe at the same time sucking down the lemon slushes—that is if she noticed at all.

Patsy Peldo growled at us when we ordered lemon slushes because the ice had to be chopped by hand, but man, they were great.

I might have had a shot with Tracy had I confessed the infatuation. Nah. The best teenage love is always unrequited. You don't have to wait for the pain that comes with the breakup. It's there in the beginning. Might as well cut to the chase.

But I always had the voices to fall back on. They spoke to me every night from KSDN Aberdeen, KSJB Jamestown, KOMA in Oklahoma City and WLS Chicago.

KSJB was king back then—in my mind at least. Bobby Gaye, Ole Olson and Wee Winnie Winslow spoke to me, assuring me that I was cool—maybe the coolest cat in the whole seventh grade and so what if Tracy Lahr never did notice me. The voices knew. We rocked together every night.

John Hruby spun stacks of wax on K-Fire (KFYR)! The Doc of Rock machine gunned intros over only the coolest of the cool songs at KSDN, firing that AM signal from nine directional towers, sizzling, directly into my brain. Eric Snow and Norm Anderson and Les Cummings were there, cool, hip and happinin', but the Doc was the coolest because you knew he "just had to be on something" and anyone that could talk that fast, even if it made no sense at all, had to be more than all right.

The voices came through car radios at night as we aimlessly drifted on gravel roads. John "Records" Landecker "boogie checked" my socks off. "And Records truly is my middle name," he would say, and I believe him still. And he, most definitely, was on something.

The voices were there at my grandparents' farm south of Gackle in the attic that was my bedroom two weeks a year while I systematically exterminated the gophers for a dime a tail from the pastures.

The Forties era console radio took forever to warm up, but it did, and then the voices would speak to me. Hurricane Smith sang to me for the first time through that radio. *Oh, Babe, What Would You Say?* he sang like Rudy Vallee through a megaphone. In time the tubes in that old radio faded and finally expired. It was not the first radio I would kill.

My moments are defined by the radio. I was watering the bushes at Sunset Memorial Gardens in Aberdeen in 1977 when the news broke. Elvis was dead. Is there a better place to be than a cemetery when you first mourn the King? The voices understood irony. And destiny.

They understood me.

We were connected by invisible tethers that reached out and skipped off the clouds from Chicago and Little Rock and Oklahoma City.

Don McClean baked *American Pie* and Isaac Hayes gave me the *Shaft.* Zager and Evans predicted ominous things for the year 2525, and I argued with Ryan Lenz that I would be around to see a future where *"you'll pick your son, pick your daughter, too, from the bottom of a long black tube. Whoa, whoa."***

We were both right—him on the point that I might make 2025 but certainly not 2525. OK, I never claimed to be a mathematician.

The voices were not infallible either. God help us, *"We had joy we had fun, we had seasons in the sun."**** I danced my first slow dance to F*eelings* in the little brown building in Barnard with Annie Oschner. There's something wrong about that—the music, I mean. Dancing your first slow dance with the amazing Annie Oschner was most certainly the right move.

But I did not hold Morris Albert and Paper Lace and Bo Donaldson and the Heywoods against the voices because they did not hold my flaws against me.

They were cool.

I was cool.

That's what the voices told me. But they never told Tracy Lahr.

© Tony Bender, 2002

* Words and Music by Lee Pockriss and Paul Vance

** Zager and Evans

*** Seasons In the Sun, (Le Moribond) (McKuen-Brel)

✎ THE WRITE STUFF

I'm not
Wayne

I heard the clatter of the teletype and was shocked by what awaited me. Wayne Lubenow had been hospitalized after a serious fall. The following updates were increasingly ominous and led to that final transmission.

And then it was over.

Somehow, I felt like calling the family, but what was there to say? I'd never met Wayne or Rosie or that large brood of a family. Still, I felt, like thousands of others, that I knew him from his columns.

If you can feel a smile at a distance, then Wayne must have been bombarded with them.

The subsequent obituaries helped flesh out the life of Wayne Lubenow. I read about his newspaper work, his war record and his battles with the bottle. Nothing surprising, really. He was just a common man with an uncommon gift.

He could communicate.

He touched people.

He once wrote, *"It's cause for elation to see one's own words in print, to float them out for all the world to read and to learn that some of the world actually does read them. Of their own free will! It warms the heart—cockles and muscles and all. On the other hand, I have learned that in spite of my frequent and sound advice, the world has not become a noticeably more peaceable kingdom. Folly abounds, incompetence waxeth, integrity waneth, nonsense prevails, thieves multiply, power corrupts. And my bones creak in the morning.*

"Still, spectacular things go on in the sky: forms and colors and movements, cloud shapes and sunscapes so awesome I ought to end every day standing on a rooftop clapping and calling for more."

I found that column, published April 10, 1991, in the **Ashley Tribune**, in a huge stack of yellow clippings my **mother had** saved. Hundreds of my columns and one of **Wayne's. She was** collecting the wrong columnist.

When I started writing this column, people wondered if I wanted to be "another Wayne Lubenow." That bothered me. Another Wayne Lubenow? No, I wanted to be the First Tony Bender! Still, the comparison was meant as a compliment, I knew. Wayne was an icon. The pinnacle of achievement would be to scale the heights of Mount Lubenow.

It's a long way to the top.

He was The Man when I started. That, I knew. But I'm not pretentious enough to believe he knew who I was. Just another pretender. But I learned from his work.

Sometimes when I find myself searching for that perfect word, trying to get too fancy, I catch myself.

"Just say it," I believe Wayne might have said.

That's what I admired about his work. Nothing fancy, simple, straight-ahead words that spoke volumes. Take it or leave it. Yet, he was eloquent:

"Slowly I learn bits of what there is to see—and then forget and learn again. And learn, too, that immortality is the stuff of life; learn how soon the young get old, how short a while forever is.

"It's sad to stand on a small hill at night and, one by one, see the lights go out around you; sad to realize you're playing the back nine; to realize there won't be time enough to get it all done— the chores, the kid-watching, the sitting on the patio to watch the birds dart at dusk, the major work.

"But there's something reassuring, too, in understanding it— death—is nature's, life's, God's way of letting up know that we were never meant to save the world singlehandedly, to keep the sun aloft and the old globe spinning."

Wayne's simple elegance reminds me of a Jerry Jeff Walker performance I saw once. I had seen him at a college concert some years before when he was riding high with a couple of hit records, a six-piece band and stacks of amplifiers.

This time, it was just Jerry, a guitar, one small amp and a

microphone. He hadn't had a hit in a long time.

And wouldn't you know, that one small amp wouldn't work. Jerry stood there as a technician fiddled with the wires for a good 10 minutes.

The silence got almost unbearable and 200 restless cowboys started to squirm. Finally, Jerry stepped up to the mike.

"Things are just gettin' too damn sophisticated," he wryly drawled. I understood his self-effacement. It was a great concert. Cut the flourishes, the bells and whistles, and get to the heart of the matter.

Wayne did that.

"What we're meant to do, I hope, is fill some small and temporary slot, to give off a little light for a little while and then lie down," he wrote.

"I'm comfortable with that, with the notion of being a small voice yapping away at the edge of a large prairie in the northern half of a small planet.

"I'm one of many voices, neither the wisest nor the best, but it's mine and fairly close to as good as I can make it."

Well, Wayne, your work is finished and ready or not, it's time to make way for the brash young Turks. It's the way of the world, and you know, Wayne, I have to believe that you were once brash and invincible too.

And before I close, I want you to know that whenever I got my hands on the paper, your column was the first thing I looked for. That's the highest compliment I can give. Now, once in a while, someone tells me the same thing.

You must have heard it a thousand times.

So now if someone mentions me in the same breath with Wayne Lubenow, I'll consider it an honor. And I will know they are damn liars.

But I hope that when I grow old and the years have brought me wisdom, when time has smoothed the rough edges, I hope that people will say to the young guns, "So you want to be another Tony Bender?"

If that happens, I'll remember you.

© Tony Bender, 1991 Revised in 2001

Ghost of
Dick Pence

We dodged each other for a dozen years or so. I would
return for the renewal of spirit that comes with a
journey to your hometown, only to find I had missed
him. Again.

"Dick Pence was just here," they would mock as they regaled
me with his latest quip, "and you missed him. Again."

This old writer was like a ghost. You heard about him. You
heard about the hauntings and the legend. You just never witnessed the apparition first hand. Everyone else knew him. I
would mention the name of this great writer from my hometown,
and invariably the response would be, "Dick Pence? Great guy.
Let me tell you about the time..."

With each stop in Frederick, Dick would leave a message
that would be passed from my mother to me. "The boy has tal-

ent," he said. "Tell him to keep writing."

In the beginning, I did not know who this ghost was. But I learned his work had appeared in national publications for years. The resume was impressively thick. *And this man thought I had something.* That was enough to get me through sometimes when I labored over a column for the *Brown County News,* the paper that had documented his accomplishments over the years.

Eventually Dick wrote to me. Or I wrote to him. And with the advent of e-mail, there have been messages which appear out of the ether.

Once, in response to a column in which I flatly stated that dogs can't count, Dick corrected me with a letter—a story really—about his dog, Brownie, who he claimed was a fair to middling mathematician.

It was a brilliant piece of writing, and he published it in his book, *Two Longs and a Short.* He prefaced the story in his letter with a complaint that Frederick folks—his own relatives, even—had begun to view me as the town's preeminent scribe.

Then came the story, so spectacularly and casually told, that the message between the lines was clear. He was still number one. The old gunslinger still had some ammo left. And he could still shoot.

• • •

When I arrived in Juneau from Denver to do a morning show at KTKU in 1986, the locals looked down their noses at me and told me about the recently retired radio legend, Uncle Fats. "That Fats... He was really something," they said. I hated Fats; even though, I never met him, and I resolved to slay him. Years later, a fresh young program director called me from KTKU. He wanted me to come back to Juneau. "Everywhere I go, I hear about Tony Bender," he said. I turned the job down. The offer had been enough. Fats was dead.

• • •

I did not wish to bury Dick Pence because with his kind encouragement—critiques from a real live professional—he marked the trail for me. But that did not stop me from enjoying his complaint about me horning in on his territory.

A few months ago, I was telling Kent Brick, editor of *North Dakota Living Magazine*, about Dick Pence's whining.

Of course, Kent knew Dick. Doesn't everyone? And Kent added that if I was indeed Frederick's most famous writer, I was certainly not the best.

Long ago, Dick and I had threatened to meet in Frederick just to see if the cosmos would explode. The plan was to drink a six pack under the water tower.

There was an all-school reunion scheduled last weekend, and Dick and I agreed that it was time to meet face to face. But something was troubling him. Why was it we were going to meet under the water tower, anyway? he wondered. I wrote back with my theory that when we scheduled this Yalta-like conference, we had assumed Frederick's population of 300 or so would have expanded, and we might get lost in the metropolis.

"Ah, a landmark." Dick wrote back.

I would be at the watertower Friday at 2 p.m., I e-mailed him.

I got this reply: "Deal. Dick."

At precisely 2 'o clock, I drove up. He was already there. I brought Budweiser, because Kent Brick told me that is what Dick drinks, and we sat under the shade of the tower, Dick in his wheelchair and me like a disciple on the ground.

Arthritis and a broken vertebrae has twisted his head cruelly downward, so you must get lower than Dick so he can see you.

We told old stories and drank the warm beer. His stories were older than mine.

I know we could have met in the air-conditioned bar, but it seemed more poetic that we should meet, broiling even in the shade, under the pale green and silver water tower. It seemed like the sort of thing writers would do.

Dick's wife and chauffeur, Ellyn, took a photo of me at Dick's feet, looking up to him, because that is the way it should be. Her southern accent is sweet as pecan pie.

When the beer was gone, and after the mayor had stopped by to see who was in violation of the open container law, we ended the visit.

But there was one issue to be resolved. Was he still king, or was I the new king? Kent Brick is an astute judge of writing, Dick told me. He would certainly not want to argue with Kent.

Hmmm.

"So how is your health?" I asked Dick.

He looked at me through the clouds in his failing eyes. I am sure he could not see me clearly. Now, I am the apparition. A spector from the future.

"Just fine," he lied.

"Then I guess I will be number two for a while longer," I said. I feel kind of bad about Fats, anyway.

© Tony Bender, 2002

Sorry about
the rock

"Lives collide," the young writer wrote later in observation of the sublime ricochet of lives, bouncing, seemingly unconnected, off one another, and then careening off into the distance, their trajectories forever altered.

Sometimes they are big crashes; other times curious, imperceptible bumps to the oblivious.

There was a big crash, two weeks into his first newspaper job in the dusty high plains town of Williston, ND, which was mired in the bust of a boom-bust oil economy. Williston is so far north and so far west, it is almost Canada and almost Montana.

The flawless 1991 Mustang with just 7,000 miles on the odometer crept unaware into a blinding rising sun past the stop sign playing hide and seek behind unpruned saplings on the boulevard.

There was the screech of tires from the three quarter ton Dodge pickup barreling to the south and then there was the crash. Metal crunched. Glass tinkled and the yellow blood leaked from the radiator.

There were subsequent crashes in the newsroom between the editor and the writer, smaller bumps, but consistent, and six months later he was gone, careening to the sanguine south in another Mustang having eulogized the departed one.

Williston isn't for everyone.

It was perfect for Bill Shemorry, who began viewing the world through the lens of a Vest Pocket Kodak camera in 1930 when he was 16. Ten years later, the moments he captured began to appear on the pages of the *Williston Press-Graphic* and when he followed his country to war as a member of the 164th Signal Photo Company, his lens discovered Chiang Kai-shek, Chou En-lai, Mao Tse-Tung and General "Vinegar Joe" Stillwell before returning to Williston and the newspaper.

Those days are gone, but the memories are vivid, and the old man who now forgets where his slippers are, remembers with clarity the defining moments along the way. He sits and listens amongst the suits and formal dresses of the 116th North Dakota Newspaper Association Banquet as his achievements are listed.

There were sixteen books. The creation of the *Williston Plains Reporter.* Photographs in national magazines and the crowning achievement in 1951—the photograph that made *Life* magazine, the picture that documented the discovery of oil that would transform a community and a state. Bill Shemorry was good at being at the right place at the right time.

It is good these inductions into the newspaper hall of fame are done for the living and not only for the dead as it used to be, the young writer thinks from his seat, having returned these 11 years later. He has maneuvered prudently around the streets of Williston this time, and so far there have been no collisions.

Tonight the younger man watches the old man who sits satisfied, reflecting on journeys past as his hands rest on his cane. He is surrounded by family members from far and wide, and beside him is Glo, proud as any wife can be.

It is good they are still here for each other, that they can be together as the conventioneers return to Williston for the first time in 28 years to the place where Bill Shemorry has made a name for himself, where he and Glo have made their modest home on a corner lot of a busy intersection where saplings grow unpruned.

A massive boulder, created eons before, once rested like a sentry in front of the house, but like so many moments and friends who have slipped away, Bill Shemorry has outlasted it.

The young writer, who is not so young anymore, rises on instinct to photograph Bill Shemorry's induction into the hall of fame. He does not know Bill or Glo, but something drives him to rise, to capture the moment which has frozen most everyone else. They sit motionless behind the bleached white tablecloths, gulping silently, fighting back the tears because they, too, recognize the moment.

The camera clicks, and Bill smiles at the once exiled writer, flashing an OK sign, his index finger meeting his thumb.

Afterward, Glo, resplendent in violet, clutches the arm of the writer to offer words of encouragement. There are those who think his work, if not great, is better than average, and she is one of those.

"I always loved your writing. But I never got to know you. You weren't here very long," she says without a hint of accusation. The writer leans closer to her and his arm loops around her like it does around his own mother. He listens and beams, glancing now and then at Bill, who is surrounded by hugs and handshakes.

"I still remember the day you came to our house after the accident," Glo says. The writer's mouth drops open.

"That was you?"

"I was probably still in my bathrobe," she continues. "It was such huge noise. I was so glad you weren't hurt."

After the collision, after the airbag and seatbelts had prevented injury or worse, the truck careened out of control into the Shemorry yard striking the boulder with such force, it split in half.

Insurance reimbursed the Shemorrys for the rock which had so admirably defended the house and prevented Bill from being pasted to the bumper along with his toast and eggs. Wouldn't that have been a kicker? You duck the bullets of WWII and succumb to a license plate imbedded in your forehead. But the Shemorrys never replaced the rock.

The writer's eyes grew wider in the wonder of it all, not

believing for a moment that all accidents are accidents. Indeed, lives collide, but sometimes you do not recognize when it has happened.

There have been collisions since—the lines crease the writer's face— and more to come. He gives Glo a hug and glances once more at the old man basking in the moment.

"I'm so sorry about the rock," I said.

© Tony Bender, 2002

Tony Dean
was there

This year it was going to be different. I pulled out all the stops. I called all the media—so often I was charged with stalking—to advise them of my booksigning.

Loyal readers (no one in Fargo, however) will recall the tale of the disastrous booksigning in that community last year during which the high falutin' Fargo media reacted to my book with a collective sigh and then lapsed into a coma.

"Disaster, Tony?" you might ask. "Isn't that a bit strong for a poor showing at a literary event?"

No, it's not! And I'd appreciate if you'd stop talking when I'm trying to write. I'm on a deadline here!

Check the newest encyclopedia under "disaster." You've got the Titanic... The Hindenburg... The Levant Bar Mitzvah when Uncle Hymie got caught with the hat check girl... And my 2000

Fargo booksigning.

I still suspect that the sign on my table did not read "Tony Bender—A Powerful New Voice From the Dakotas" like it was supposed to. This one, I remain convinced, said "CAUTION, LEPER WITH INFECTIOUS WEEPING SORES!"

But back to the future which is now the past. Still stinging from the poor turnout, I put a full court press on the press.

I sent the *Fargo Forum* three books! After sending the first one, I followed up with Tammy Swift, the lifestyles editor (and a terrific columnist) to make sure she had the book.

Didn't get it.

So I sent another.

And another.

Finally, three weeks later, she got all three books—signed, of course. Some mail room they've got there. So it turned out I signed more books for the *Fargo Forum* than I did at the signing.

Of course there would not be time to do a review of the book before I came to town. Shafted. Screwed. Scammed. Chagrined. Broke-down and busted.

Bogus.

When I checked the *Fargo Forum* entertainment calendar the week of my big event, it announced that Tony Dean, the legendary Dakota sportsman, would be in town to sign his new book, "The Great and Mighty Da-Da."

Really. That's what it said. Tony Dean.

So I e-mailed Tammy Swift to complain.

"Dear Tommy...

But even on the day of the signing, I was listed in media outlets as Tony Dean.

However, the *High Plains Reader* put my photo right under Ozzy Osborne's and right beside Snoop Dogg's. That was the concert where they arrested all those folks on firearms possession charges. There were lots of guns at my signing, too, but mostly because they wanted to show Tony Dean their special goose gun.

If you can't beat 'em, join 'em. Instead of regaling the audience, which had traipsed in wearing all sorts of hunter orange and tan camouflage, with stories from my stunningly brilliant new book, I gave them huntin' and fishin' tips.

When I demonstrated my fly casting technique, invented on the spot, I hooked the ear lobe of the guy behind the coffee bar.

"That ain't how you do it," one guy, sitting in a tree stand, drawled.

"Hey, Goober! Who's giving the demonstration here?"

"You are."

"And what's my name?"

"Tony Dean."

"Damn straight. Now, sit down and listen! You might learn something."

As a tribute to Ozzy, I bit the head off a pheasant, a technique that was duly recorded in notebooks as a new method to clean wild game. The incident was captured by a local TV station, lured to the store by the idea of capturing the great Tony Dean on video for a news feature.

114

I was dabbing at the pheasant blood on my shirt when a man hurried in.

"Would you sign my sausage?"

"Beg your pardon?"

"And then could you sing, *Big, Bad John?* I really love the part where the mine collapses on him."

"I'm sorry," I said. "You're thinking of Jimmy Dean—I'm Tony Dean."

"Oh," he said.

I was pretty pumped up to see the TV piece. I was trying to imagine what they'd say..."Tonight at 10, madman and outdoorsman Tony Dean presents new wild game cleaning techniques..."

But the story got bumped. Seems there were quintets born in Fargo—five of them, which made it really big news—so old Tony Dean got shelved.

© Tony Bender, 2001

✍ THE OLD MAN AND THE ME

Shaving
cream

I got the bowling shirts. They were gaudy things in unfortu-
nate colors, but his name was embroidered on the pockets,
so I took them, hangers and all, from the closet.

And shaving cream. I got shaving cream. Different brands.
Varied scents. But every one of them had a discount sticker. The
man could not walk by a red tag no matter if it was minced ham
beginning to turn green or discounted shaving cream. My father
loved to save a buck.

It was laughable that I should get the shaving cream because
I hate the process so. I shave for weddings. I shave for funerals.
But barring such catastrophes, I grow a beard and when it gets
ragged, a month or so later, I shave it off. Shaving cream lasts a
long time around here.

But slowly, over the nine years, I went through the cans,

watching the changes in the mirror.

Scrape. Scrape. Watch the creases deepen. Scrape. Scrape away the heartache. Scrape. Damn, I cut myself again.

I gave the bowling shirts to The Redhead's mother and though it doesn't seem right, I forgot about them until she brought them back to me just before Christmas. She had turned them into Teddy Bears. One read "McKay Elevator." The other said "Frederick Equity Exchange" and they both had "Norm" embroidered on the front.

Scrape. Scrape away the years. Scrape. Watch my hairline recede. Scrape. Study the scars.

I gave the Teddy Bears to my sisters for Christmas. Sherry opened the box, bit her lip and then walked out of the room, not looking at me. Not looking at anyone.

She was soaking up the tears with a tissue when I walked into the kitchen, the din and excitement of the children shredding wrapping paper behind us.

She could not speak. She just sobbed as she flung her arms around me. I was not crying. I must not cry. Enough time has passed. I cannot mourn anymore. But my eyes will not listen.

The last can got so corroded it left stains on the sink every time I used it, the rusty circles matching the orange design on the Colgate can. Regular scent.

I wondered if I would empty it before it rusted through. The can clung tenuously to life, wheezing out more foam each time I needed it.

Scrape. I have to lean closer to the mirror now. My eyes are weak. Scrape. Mustn't dawdle. Dylan needs to get to school and India must go to day care. Scrape. Sigh.

Fleeting thoughts had come and gone as the can faded, but I dismissed them. Pretending it was just another old rusty can coughing out the last of the shaving cream.

Scrape. It's just a can of shaving cream for goodness sakes! Scrape. No big deal, really. Scrape. Move on, already, will you! Scrape.

Half an hour before the meeting, I aimed the nozzle into my palm. It spat. It sputtered out a small dollop of foam, and then it was done.

I shaved slowly, carefully. Don't want to bleed to death in a room full of strangers.

Scrape. I hope my presentation goes well. Scrape. Probably should have rehearsed. Scrape. Aww, there's something to be said for spontaneity, I guess. Scrape.

When I was done, I swept my toothbrush into the shaving kit along with the aftershave and toothpaste. Ten minutes to go. Better get dressed.

As I was walking out, I grabbed the can and tossed it into the empty wastebasket. The rattle echoed loudly off the cold tile, and it made me stop.

It didn't seem right that the end should come like this. There should be something more. Some sort of ceremony. A little more respect. Something.

I pulled the can back out and cradled it almost reverently in both hands, and I felt the warmth from the invisible touch starting on my shoulder and enveloping me, causing me to smile. A wistful sort of smile.

I studied the can for a moment longer and then set it softly back on the bathroom sink.

I glanced into the bathroom as I rushed out with my bags and hangers. I stopped at the door of Room 231 and turned, like I always do, to see if I had forgotten anything. To see if I had left anything behind. I am never quite sure.

Then I closed the door firmly behind me.

© Tony Bender, 2001

You're not
going like that

Getting ready for an outing at our house was always sublimely comedic.

Mom would answer queries as to the whereabouts of socks and shirts for six kids, clipping on earrings with one hand, brushing the hair of a child with the other.

We'd be zipping up parkas when Dad would appear, whistling *Sweet Georgia Brown*, wearing his old paint-stained elevator pants. His T-shirt had been washed so many times, and was so thin and full of holes, you couldn't net minnows with it.

Clad in our Sunday best, we'd stare and nudge each other knowingly. Then Mom would materialize from the bathroom. That's when it would start.

"Norman, you are not going like that."

"What's wrong with this?" he'd ask, pretending to have the I.Q. of a goat. While the litany of fashion flaws were rattled off, we'd unzip our coats, resigned to a 15-minute wait.

It always ended the same. Dad, feelings wounded, would trudge back up the stairs for another try. Sometimes he'd have to change two or three times before Mom would let him out of the house. I was never sure just how bad his fashion sense was. Oh, it was bad all right. I mean Blackwell sent him weekly hate mail. But I always suspected that he'd cackle to himself alone in the closet thinking, "I bet if I wear plaids and stripes, she'll go through the roof."

One day, as Mom and Dad prepared for a trip to his hometown of Ashley, he came down in his usual Pa Kettle finery. Mom took one look and said, "Wait just a minute."

When she reappeared, she was wearing an awful faded, baggy, stained, yellowish sweatshirt, pink polyester slacks and paint-spattered tennis shoes.

"You're not going like that!" Dad blustered after he caught his breath.

"Why not? We'll match."

"I'm not taking you looking like that."

He must have driven around the block once or twice before coming back to see if she'd come to her senses.

"Well, are you going to change?"

Nope. She wasn't giving in.

"So he left me!" Mom laughs.

© Tony Bender, 1996

A new
tacklebox

The gleaming tan and green tacklebox beckoned. It was on sale. I'd never actually bought a tacklebox. The two tackleboxes I'd owned before had been hand-me-downs from my father.

The first was a small, steel box, spray-painted green to hide the scars. I used it for years. But somewhere along the miles of my life, it was discarded.

The tacklebox I'd been using until this year was my father's last one. It rested, dusty and spotted by oil, in the garage, so I took it home with me.

It was bursting with tackle. Hooks and rigs for every type of freshwater fish in the Midwest. The irony of this impressive collection did not escape me. I smiled. I chuckled. You see, my father, the man with this intimidating tangle of spinners, daredevils, bobbers and lead weights, rarely fished.

I think we fished together—maybe a half dozen times. There just never seemed to be enough time.

But the tacklebox spoke volumes about Dad's optimism. One day he would fish for weeks on end. He would snag dozens of hooks on sunken logs. Lunkers would snap leaders. And he would be prepared.

I took that tacklebox with me every year on my annual fishin' trip with the boys up on the Continental Divide of Colorado. But when I added my trout gear to the box, it began to bulge. A search for a #10 snelled hook could last minutes.

Like my father, I could not pass by the aisles of fishing gear without purchasing some new wonder bait or guaranteed spinner.

So I bought the gigantic new tacklebox. It boasted drawers and compartments enough for two fishermen.

I waited till the last day before I was to leave on this men-only trip to transfer the gear from Dad's old tacklebox to my new one.

I didn't expect it to become a ritual, but it did as I lovingly stored all of my father's paraphernalia.

The Redhead urged me to finish the task. It was her last chance to get some work out of me for a week. But the ritual had become religion and each hook safely stored, a prayer.

I tucked the old, empty tacklebox into the closet. The Redhead plans to use it to decorate Dylan's room. And when he is older, it will go back into service.

The boys found a new lake this year. Surrounded by fragrant

pines and crumbling granite mountains, the waters gleamed as flawless as a mirror in the orangish early morning light.

As we sat on the shore in dawn's radiant silence, two moose emerged from the shadowed forest and splashed noisily across the lake to graze choice rushes.

As we watched, Bob spoke inspired words. "This is good for the soul." Fishing is religion.

Fishing was fair—better than last year—and I was the leading fisherman.

On the last day, when our luck had run out, I reeled in my line. Then I felt a tug. Surprised, I didn't set the hook well. I reeled the 10 inch trout closer to shore, and he darted bravely between the rocks, fighting for his life. Then, as Tom lowered the net, the fish slipped off the hook. Tom strained to find the fish, hoping to net him before he reached deeper water. Silently, curiously, I cheered for the trout. With a sassy swish of his tail and a last sparkling gleam of rainbow scales, he disappeared.

I packed my gear. I felt a few pangs of guilt as I glanced at that new tacklebox, as if leaving that old tacklebox behind had been a betrayal. But I silenced the guilt with my rationalizations. The many remaining empty drawers are a testament to *my* optimism. I will fill them. And I will fish. Dad, your tacklebox didn't make the trip this year. But you did.

© Tony Bender, 1997

Norm's garden

March clings tenuously to winter with snowy, diamond fingers gripping the plain. But with Easter's approach I think of spring.

When I think of Easter, I think of lilies.

When I think of spring, I think of the hues of green in May.

And when I think of May, I think of him.

He would have been 56 in May.

"Well, I made 55," he said matter-of-factly last May 1.

Even as he lay on sterile white hospital sheets, we planned memorials. There would be a garden in the back yard, Mom decided. So in his winter, we prepared for spring. We carefully selected dwarf trees and shrubs. And bulbs were planted among the petunias. A ceramic birdbath welcomed feathered visitors.

In a time of powerlessness, Norm's Garden provided diversion from pain.

It provided peace.

It was a garden of acceptance. A memorial to the living we knew would not breathe much longer.

Across the street, Bill industriously cleared the abandoned lot he'd purchased. He explained why he was digging up a flower bed along the street, so far from his window, closer to our house than his. The idea sprouted from a talk he'd had with my father on a sunny day the year before, on Bill's porch.

Dad had trucked for several years, hauling the prairie's amber harvest to Minneapolis, and his journeys had led him through a striking little Minnesota town. There, the community planted flowers along the roadways.

It was a magnificent sight.

"Why couldn't people around here do that?" he wondered.

So Bill was trimming hedges and planting flowers.

The daily news we brought back from the hospital was not encouraging but, "Norm's got to rally one more time to see the flowers," burly Bill told my mother.

My father had rallied so many times before.

So there were two gardens separated by asphalt.

A garden of acceptance and a garden of hope.

We needed them both.

But before May was over, and before the first blooms, the struggle ended. So we marked the progress of the flowers through the summer, and we watched them shrivel in the frosts of autumn.

But this year, flowers will bloom again. Spectacular, delicate, resilient color will touch us once again with the rebirth.

Even as the harshest winter grips futilely to the soil, the sprouts plan their summer victory.

My mind goes back to the blooms.

I think of Easter and I think of Norm's Garden.

I think of flowers that will once again greet the living.

I remember Dad and I think of spring.

© Tony Bender, 1994

✍ OUT OF MY LEAGUE

Where Teddy
Ballgame is

I never saw the greatest hitter that ever lived play. He retired when I was two. So why do I care? I care because I respected the way he lived. If Ted Williams did not write the song, "My Way," he should have.

But he drummed out a beat of line drives and homeruns that had not been seen before—not since Ty Cobb anyway—or since.

In 1939—and this story has been told a million times but what are good stories if they cannot be retold—Ted Williams was a rookie with the Red Sox. Rookies are supposed to be awed. Williams was, well, Williams, and if he was awed, it was over his own abilities with a stick.

In spring training, the baseball writer Al Horwitz said to Williams, "Wait till you see Jimmy Foxx hit."

"The rookie gazed out the window dreamily. His fingers

gripped the handle of an imaginary bat," the great Red Smith wrote of that moment.

"Wait," Williams said, "until Foxx sees me hit."

Indeed.

He was cantankerous. Disdainful of the lessers who could not fathom the greatness. When the Red Sox fans booed him after a lackadaisical play, Teddy Ballgame dug in. Him against the world. And he held the grudge, spitting at the press box, flipping off the fans and refusing to acknowledge the cheers when he was great—and that was most of the time—with a tip of the hat.

When he batted .406 he refused to tip his hat. When he returned from WWII and Korea, he refused to tip his hat. When he hit a homerun in his last at bat when he was 42, the year he batted .316, he would not give in.

And now the 83-year-old, stroke-ravaged shell of Ted Williams lies in a vat of liquid nitrogen in the desert. No one knows for sure at this point if it was Ted's idea or not. But it sure sounds a lot like a man who would not give in—ever. It sounds like a man who unabashedly sought immortality. This is the stuff of Gods.

But Atlas has faded away. Neptune is gone. And Hercules. But we remember them still. And some days, the sunshine is interrupted by thunderbolts above, and we know that Zeus is still out there, rattling the skies.

But they will not come back here again. And even if some future mad scientist can start the valves and the pumps working in a thawed corpse, that will not be Ted Williams.

Ted Williams is out there somewhere. Up there. He is up above; even though, he would not acknowledge God because Ted could not imagine one greater than himself.

By now, that's all been straightened out. Even the great Ted Williams could not dig in so firmly that he could not step back to avoid the brush back pitch. Ted Williams, brash, a man's man, always had the ability to step back and see things as they really were. He might not admit it. But he could see. Any man who could count the seams of a 90 mph fastball most certainly could see as much as we lessers could.

It was 31 years after that final homerun that Ted Williams returned to Fenway Park. It was 1991, and he still had the stride and the gaze of a confident man. When he was introduced, he stepped up and smiled. Then he pulled that hat off his head and held it high.

If you listen, you can still hear the cheers. Listen closer, and you can hear the crack of the bat and the whistle of the ball driven disdainfully past the Lou Boudreau shift into right field for a clean single.

Listen. The sound is still there, rippling out like a splash into a calm pond. Close your eyes and you can still see him. Slim. Quick wrists. Quick smile. He is there, immortal already.

Zeus is pitching lightning bolts. Ted Williams is at the plate. St. Peter whispers from behind the plate. "Wait till you see God hit," he says as Williams takes the first pitch, a fastball a half inch off the plate.

"Wait 'till God sees me hit," Ted says as he bangs the next one over the fence. The crowd cheers. Even God, on deck, batting cleanup, applauds.

Williams hesitates.

Then he reaches up to the brim of his hat and tips it.

That is where Ted Williams is.

© Tony Bender, 2002

The one I wasn't going to write

This year I wasn't going to write a baseball column. I broke the same vow last year...

But as dawn's light crept through the blinds this morning, my mind was filled with the images again.

How do you explain it—the force that turns the wheel—that makes it nearly impossible to drive by a Little League game on a summer's day?

You might as well seek an answer to the force that pulls magnets together, that holds planets in orbit, that draws the geese to the north when snows release their grip.

It's not about scientific explanations because when you break it down, the answer is always the same—it's magic. And baseball is magic.

So last summer when I was coming home to visit, I was a scant 16 miles away when I saw the championship combatants warming up outside the fence. And the wheel turned, I swear, of its own accord.

Two dollars gets you a parking place down the right field line where your car stands flinching at the whistling foul balls of the cleanup batter. Yes, and two dollars buys you a spot behind home plate. Another dollar gets you a Coke and Fischer's sunflower seeds.

Three dollars buys a spot among friends where wrinkling grandmothers harangue volunteer umpires over ball and strike calls. Three dollars buys a sunburn and memories.

Memories of the centerfielder who was me, in near ecstasy on a burning July morning chasing batting practice flies with such fervor that his coach had to almost drag him to the hose for a drink. Memories of a tilt-kneed Tony Oliva in his final season at the Met, still driving the ball with authority past diving shortstops. Memories of summer days in Mile High Stadium when the Denver Bears ruled from April to September.

It's funny, the things your memory captures. But every year I think of the grandfather and the adoring grandson, both in their Bears caps, who sat directly in front of me one day.

I remember the silent looks they exchanged after the spectacular Barry Larkin throw from deep in the hole. The impassive look from the old one, the grin of the young, hot dog forgotten for the moment. That I remember. The score is forgotten.

It's more than the game itself. It's the halter tops and the behind the back toss of the peanut vendor to the 23rd row. And if he misfires, he asks for the bag back and another try.

I remember bringing my own grandfather to the park the day we finagled a box seat. He sat wide-eyed, with a clean, new cap of his own, far removed from his Dakota farm, hot dog and beer in his hands. "I feel chust like a king," he said.

That's baseball. It's magic.

Then the rumble of the crowd brings the little league game back into focus. The visitors are one hit away from a rally. The hometown boys are just an out away from a trophy.

The number eight hitter goes down swinging. I remember the player I knew so intimately doing the same against our despised rivals from Barnard.

A whiff to end the game on our home field.

But as the boy walks away to the consolations of Dad and to the silence of teammates, I continue my journey home with the peace of knowing in my heart. I know that another day the bat will connect and an inside-the-parker will win the game.

There is always redemption on the green gopher-holed field. Even peanut venders get another chance. It's baseball. It's spring. And it's magic.

© Tony Bender, 1994

Writer's note: My friend, Bob, has the greatest job in the world. He's a radio engineer for the sports teams who visit Denver. So he works with all the great announcers. Marv Albert. The late Chick Hearn. Harry Carey.

A *Twins fan from way back, Bob was thrilled to work with Herb Carneal a few years ago. Halsey Hall is long gone, but Carneal shared a story with Bob about the inimitable Hall. The duo was on the road and the engineer didn't have the kind of hand-held microphone Halsey preferred. But the engineer dug around and came up with a small round hand-held mike a little larger than a silver dollar. "Between innings," Herb recalled, "Halsey would set the mike down. When we'd get back on the air, he'd pick it up."*

After one inning, Carneal looked over and "there was Halsey, doing play-by-play, holding a stop watch to his lips!"

They're killing my game

Writer's note: I love the game, but sometimes the changes make me wanna scream. So I scream.

Ping! I hate it. Ping! That's the sound of the bat at Little League games today.

From the bleachers we drink our colas from earth-killing plastic, we eat hot dogs rumored to contain actual meat as well as 97 percent preservatives that may well allow the wieners to outlast the plastic, and we watch as the eighth man in the line-up knocks a check-swing off the handle over the fence which is so close, you feel like you're back in prison.

OK, so maybe that last part is just me. And I can live with it all except for that infernal ping of the aluminum bat.

Anyone who has read this column for these past dozen years knows that like clockwork, every year I must publish another ode to baseball. Maybe it's because I still believe it's the great American pastime. Maybe it's because it's the only sport for which I ever showed an inkling of aptitude. But this year, there will be no ode to the scratching and spitting and strawberries suffered with a perfect slide into second.

I'm old school.

I'm so old school, I didn't walk uphill both ways to school in a blizzard. Blizzards hadn't even been invented yet. Methusala was still a pup when I went to school. I'm telling you, I'm old school. We watched dinosaurs from the window. Every boy ran a thin white cord to his ear from the transistor radio in his pocket during the World Series while teachers pretended not to notice or just gave in and asked what the score was.

I mourned the day the American League brought in the designated hitter. I still remember the first one—Ron Blomberg of the Yankees. That was April 6, 1973, and I was barely in high school, but I remember it because that is the day the world went to hell in a handbasket.

Nobody wants to see pitchers hit, they said. Yeah, well, they didn't survey me. I was a Baltimore Orioles fan, and I was used to watching Mark Belanger cover three counties at shortstop while hitting .182. Some days I wouldn't have minded if Earl Weaver pinch-hit Dave McNally for Belanger.

Nowadays, put an aluminum bat in his hand, and Belanger would still bat .200.

Just .200, Tony?

Yeah, just .200. But that's only because he's been dead since '98.

Ron Blomberg remains a suspect.

Now our Little League Belangers are all batting .400 and infielders are doomed men.

I love homeruns. Love 'em. But when little Tommy, who has been bulking up all summer on Nintendo and Skittles, jacks one over the 310 mark—Ping!—there's something terribly wrong with my game.

I have fought it. I did not want to become one of *them.* An old fogey, complaining about kids today and how things used to be better in the good old days. But I can't take it anymore. Get me to a rocking chair quick, so I can start complaining.

In my day, we hit our homeruns the old fashioned way—into the cavernous gap between center field and right. The ball would roll to the fence, which was 385 feet away—a manly distance—and you would run like a scared rabbit around the bases while the outfielders converged to dig the ball out of a gopher hole.

The relay would come in as you were chugging around third past a windmilling coach, and you would slide under the tag. Safe! Your teammates mobbed you because it was, after all, quite a feat while you strolled, nonchalant, past the sulking catcher, pretending that this was something you did every day.

Now, mutants who would have frightened Dick Butkus, jab needles filled with the same stuff they put into the hot dogs, into their buttocks and hit fifty taters in an off year.

They're taking away my game. Baseball used to be for the regular guys. The behemoths played football. The tall guys played hoops. And the Mark Belangers of the world played baseball.

I don't have time on this deadline for my rant, and the newspapers don't have the space.

But I've given up anyway. I no longer watch the game. I long-since gave up clipping and pasting every Orioles box score into my scrapbook. If any team could use steroids, it's them.

The sacred records are falling, but I cannot believe them.

Too many needles.

I wanted to believe in McGwuire, and I did, but the andro made me uneasy. I want to believe in Bonds, but I cannot. The game has been sullied by rotten owners who pretend that they give a rip about the fan.

Don't get caught in the stampede as they rush to check out this steroid issue. Don't concern yourself with 14-year-olds starting the day with a needle so they can make the team and forever lose sight of their testicles.

Bud Selig pretends to be commissioner, while putting a team so horrid on the field, my Orioles could beat them. And then, that very team is the most profitable in baseball.

Out in Minnesota, where they bounce triples off Hefty bags on artificial turf in a dome where pop-ups get lost forever, that is where the purest baseball is being played these days. So naturally, the lords of the diamond want to shut them down.

There can be no ode to baseball this year. I'm going to take my five pound bag of Fischer sunflower seeds, and I'm going to sit at the bleachers, and even though there is no game going on, I will watch in my mind's eye. I will hear the crack of the bat, *the crack*, mind you, and the groan of the crowd as it goes just foul.

Then I will stomp past the flickering Nintendo machines to my rocker.

Mark Belanger, we need you.

Come back!

© Tony Bender, 2002

Down slope

Five years and 40 pounds later, I was a little leary about getting back on a pair of skis.

But every day for a week, Jeff and Phil came into my office to harass me into hitting the slopes.

Unfortunately, I'd sold my skis before leaving Alaska. That's where I'd learned to ski.

On the many occasions when I would come flailing down that mountain outside of Juneau, tumbling and scattering ski gear for hundreds of yards, the Jamaican lift operator would offer critiques when I finally arrived at his station: "Nice tumble, mon."

Anyway, by Friday, I was still undecided about testing my 'ski legs.' But on Saturday, I found my self looking at skis. Forty-five minutes and $500 later I had my skis. Now I was locked in.

Sunday morning found me with the boys strapping on gear outside the lodge. My first injury came while trying to buckle my boots. I pulled a muscle in my right shoulder.

My plan was to find the bunny hill and take a few gentle slopes just to see if I remembered the faintest concept of skiing. But seconds after slapping the skis on, I found myself in the lift line with my cohorts.

On the way up, I reminded them that it had been five years since I'd been on skis. It had been three for Jeff and eight since Phil had skied. At that point we started discussing insurance policies. We really did.

I began to realize that it would be a minor miracle if we could dismount without one of us suffering a major skewering by our poles.

My first run was nearly my last. As I headed down the slope, I looked up and saw a snowmobile roaring toward me. I swerved. So did he. IN THE SAME DIRECTION! We both swerved again. And again we were on a collision course.

You know what it's like when you meet someone in a narrow hall and you both step to the same side? Then you step, in unison, to the other side? I call it the *Politeness Dance*.

Well, my situation with the snowmobile was like that except that this crash would likely result in my death. Death, in these circumstances, is often fatal. I managed to escape—narrowly—while getting close enough to see the pores on the driver's nose.

Meanwhile, Phil had decided that the best way to find his way down the hill was to follow the best looking female skier.

That plan, however, led him down Grim Reaper Trail. When I caught up to Phil, he was wrapped around a telephone pole at the bottom of the hill.

Now, a normal man would extricate himself from the pole, pull the slivers out of his face and vow never again to slap boards on his feet. Not Kamikaze Phil. The man wanted to do it again. I figure he has a death wish. Either that or some kind of hormonal imbalance. Maybe both.

Anyway, it was clear early on that I was not going to keep up with Jeff, an accomplished skier, or Phil, an accomplished mani-ac.

I managed to give them the slip and ended up on a lift with a dad and two first-grade girls. One of the girls fell as we loaded but I managed to catch her, amazingly, without dropping my poles. She didn't miss a beat, and we chatted on the way up the hill. A dog had bitten off part of her lip, she told me, a fact she was fairly proud of. "That's nice," I said.

On the dismount she fell under my feet. I couldn't get off without skiing over her, so I found myself heading back down the hill in the chair, looking sheepishly at the passengers coming up the hill. Like some idot with nothing better to do than ride the chair lift all day.

In retrospect, I should have taken out the kid.

Six hours later I met the boys back in the parking lot where I had been paging through the Sunday paper for the past hour.

Their mood was boisterous and many of their limbs unin-jured and accounted for. Half an hour later as we drove home,

Phil was still pulling snow from the nether regions of his ski pants, Jeff was asleep in the back seat and I was fighting cramps in my arches.

I suppose we're going to do it again.

© Tony Bender, 1994

✍ TRAVELIN' MAN

Oh
Canada

One of my duties as a columnist is to experience new
things so you, the Pringles munching couch sloth, may
live vicariously through me.

So you see, my recent trip to Canada was for your own good,
and the fact that writing about it makes it entirely tax-deductible
under Canadian law is merely a coincidence. Besides, if you
think any vacation with four children, two of whom are not
mine, is some sort of vacation, you are sadly mistaken and
should be flogged. In fact, let us pause while you slap yourself.
(Oh, that's gonna leave a mark.)

My point is, lots of research went into this column, much of
it obtained by depositing pocket change into the hands of pan-
handlers outside Place Louis Riel in Winnipeg in exchange for
information. First question: Who is Louis Riel? Answer: "Some

guy. That'll be a quarter, please."

But we did not donate just to get information. We donated because we are naive Americans. The Redhead gave one woman, who spoke fluent German, $2.50 for bus fare back home to Pine Ridge, only to find her still on the corner two days later because (a) the public transportation in Winnipeg is suspect or (b) it was a trick.

But, we got a receipt, so the $2.50 is tax deductible. Besides, the donation was in Canadian, so if you take the exchange rate into consideration, we're only out 2.7 yen. We called Arthur Andersen to verify the math.

Another little-known fact we discovered is that Canada is the 51st state. However, under the Patriot Act, that information is classified and besides you and me, only John Ashcroft knows.

I was a little nervous crossing into Canada because in 1989 I was ticketed in Saskatchewan by a Canadian Mountie with a Scottish accent and did not pay the fine because what were they gonna do? Extradite me from Myrtle Beach?

"Did ye new ye were goin' 140 kilomo-tears an are?" the mountie asked me.

"Is that good or bad?" I asked.

Luckily, Saskatchewan does not share outstanding warrant information with Manitoba. In fact, they're not even speaking. Because Saskatchewan was dating Manitoba's sister, Alberta, and for absolutely no reason at all, Manitoba stopped calling. "He just used me to get to my mountains!" Alberta wailed. But that's a whole 'nother story.

However, crossing into Canada did provide some dicey moments because we did not know the secret handshake. So we were asked all sorts of questions like were we carrying any handguns, tobacco and did we play hockey—even a little.

"Yes, I said. "In fact, my father named me for Maurice 'The Rocket' Richard."

"But," she said, studying my drivers license, "it says your name is Tony Bender."

"Yes," I said. "Dad was a notoriously bad speller."

"Hmm," she said, pointing to the back where Cheetos were in mid-flight and faces were grotesquely pressed Quasimodo-like, up against the glass. "And all of these children are yours?"

"I've never seen them before in my life," I said. "If you want we can just leave them here until we get back."

The children enjoyed Canada but were a little disappointed that the window to the twenty-third floor of Place Louis Riel did not open so they could spit out.

No vacation would be complete without history, and let me tell you, Winnipeg has just about cornered the market on history.

Our cab driver informed us the first night that the Golden Boy, the statue that has graced the dome of the Manitoba Legislative Building since 1920, has been removed for reconstruction and gilding.

Just hearing the word gilding makes me nervous because it sounds an awful lot like something they do to horses (which is a

155

free medical process in Canada). Statue gilding involves taking small, tissue-thin leaves of gold and applying it to the statue with a brush and what appears to be saliva. I know because I saw it myself.

I also learned several facts about Golden Boy. For instance, he never played for Vince Lombardi, but he would have been good because he stands four meters tall and weighs 1,650 kilograms which translates to 13.5 feet high while tipping the scales at 457 yen. The Golden Boy was sculpted in France, the same people who brought you the Statue of Liberty.

My son, Dylan, was impressed by all this when I told him.

"When we get back to Fargo, can we go to Chuck E. Cheeses?" he said.

I would have learned more historical facts about our magnificent fifty-first state, but I ran out of quarters.

I can tell you one thing, though. Canadian beer is very strong. Lethal, almost. Never consume four Canadian beers before supper and then let the waitress talk you into a whole bottle of Australian Shiraz no matter how cute and charming she is and no matter how good the exchange rate is.

That was at the Liberty Grill, which has a near-lifesize replica of the Statue of Liberty right in the restaurant. (In fact, it may be the actual Statue of Liberty, which might explain why American authorities won't let anyone near Ellis Island nowadays. Canada has stolen our statue! Don't be surprised if they take it to a chop shop, file off the serial numbers, slap some gold and spit on it and claim they got it from a second-hand shop in

Quebec.)

I had the lamb.

The Redhead had a headache. The next day is kind of a blur. I think it involved the zoo, a playground with excruciatingly squeaky swings, cold compresses to the forehead and lots of moaning. But I really don't want to get into that.

I have one more piece of advice. Never attempt to smuggle Cohibas back into the states by placing them in a condom and swallowing them just because you saw it in a movie once. Even if you have free healthcare, don't do it.

On the other hand, call me if you need a deal on cigars. They should be, uh, delivered tomorrow. Thursday, at the latest.

© Tony Bender, 2002

The trouble with Scandinavians

Let this be a warning to you. Hanging out with a bunch of Scandinavians for a week is no trifling matter. Even if you're a hardened Finlander, Norsk Hostfest in Minot is not for the faint of heart. But for a German-Russian... well... let's just say, I was lucky to survive.

I wrangled the invitation myself from a Hostfest ambassador who attended a newspaper convention last spring and saw my book, *Loons in the Kitchen*, on display. She told me she was looking for authors of Scandinavian descent.

"Is Bender Scandinavian?" she asked.

"Of course," I lied. "Got more Scands in the family than you can shake a lefse at. And my wife is too."

"Where's her family from?"

"Daneland."

"Daneland?"

"Sure. You've got Finland, Lapland, Iceland, Daneland and Swedeland."

"I see. Does your book have anything in it about Scandinavians?"

"Oh, sure," I said. (And I wasn't lying either because if you arrange the letters correctly, you can spell Norwegian in virtually every story.)

"Besides," I said. "I know lots of Finnish swear words."

I think that clinched it. For a small fee of all my worldly possessions, I was invited to the show.

Security was tight. When I showed up at the front door to unload, I did not have the proper credentials so I was detained.

"Whatcha got der, Sven," one guard asked the other. "Terrorist?"

"Vorse," said Sven. "German-Russian."

"Vell, vat shall we do wit him?" Nils asked. "Toss him in da clink ant trow away da key?"

"Dat wood be too easy, I tink," Sven said. "Look, Kraut," he said to me, "you cot two choices. We log you up ant trow away da key or you eat lutefisk, and iff you liff, we let you go."

That's when I made the biggest mistake of my life—aside from the purple Gremlin.

I ate a generous portion of the lutefisk which resembled coagulated snot. Except it didn't taste that good.

It never actually digested. It just sort of stayed there like a diseased internal organ.

I learned later, from an authentic Norwegian lady from Norland, that the best lutefisk is the old-fashioned kind that is dried first on the docks.

She remembers dogs coming along and urinating on some of the drying fish. She expressed her concerns about that to her father, a fisherman.

"Don't vorry," he said. "Dat's da stuff ve send to Sweden!"

I'll never know if the dried lutefisk really is better. I would rather eat a plate of hissing cockroaches. I know the survival rate would be higher, anyway.

One of the highlights of the event for me was having a table right around the corner from the stage. So for three days straight, I got to hear Williams and Ree, The Scandinavian and the White Guy, do the same comedy act, The Trilogy. Most folks went to all the shows because it takes that long for your average Norwegian to get the punch line.

It was quite an experience. Dennis Ihringer, a publisher, summed it up. "I've never seen so many tall, pale white people in one spot before," he said.

It got me thinking. Though I sold a fair amount of books, next year I'm gonna get rich.

I'm setting up a tanning bed.

© Tony Bender, 2001

Cream can
memory

The call came in the summer when the furnace was hunkered down in seasonal retirement and the lawn, a jungle crisis.

I didn't know the man, but he told me he had something I might be interested in. My grandfather's old cream can.

"Still has the brass plate with his name."

"John Spilloway?"

"No, Helko Spilloway."

My great-grandfather. I never met him but in the last few years of his life, I was able to prod Grandpa John to tell a few stories about his father.

You bet I wanted the can. To have a piece of my great-grandfather's life...that would be a real treasure. But it had been such a hectic summer... I tucked the phone number in my pocket where it disappeared like a fugitive sock in the dryer.

Last Saturday brought a reprieve from the tentacles of winter that had begun to grasp the countryside. Defiant sunshine caressed golden leaves in the delicate balance between frost and sunburn. The perfect day for an adventure.

I started down the list of Wolfs in the phone book. In 10 minutes I had the right one, courtesy of a helpful wrong number.

"My boy and I will be there around one," I told Doc.

I don't think I'd been back to Gackle since Grandpa John's funeral. Life's funny that way. You lose someone, and sometimes you lose a whole town right along with them.

Dylan marched right into Doc and Dee's A-frame and perched on the recliner. "We're here for the cream can," he chirped.

It was a short drive to the family homestead where the can rested in a dusty corner of the immaculately painted little red barn.

The tiny farmhouse, likewise, was wrapped in a fresh coat of paint, acres of manicured lawn spread out under it like a fading green rug. Down the hill, a wooden dock rested on shore by the pond.

To Dee and Doc's delight, Dylan slipped off his shirt to feel the sun's rays on his pale skin. In just his second autumn he recognized the opportunity as rare. I stopped him from pulling his pants off, too.

Dee let him stomp through her flower garden where blossoms inexplicably still bloomed bravely. I moved to stop Dylan

162

from picking the flowers, but Dee assured me it was all right. "They'll be gone soon enough," she said.

In the spring it might be a sin, but in the autumn it's all right to stomp through a flower garden out here among friends.

Maybe in our autumns, we ought to stomp through a few flower gardens. They'll be gone soon enough...

An immense white boulder rested in the center of the flowers. "Cost me a pretty penny," Doc smiled, the way a man out here in the plains can smile at his own foibles.

I looked at the rock. Six and a half feet tall. Maybe seven. Almost as big around as a Volkswagen. And weight? I couldn't begin to calculate the tons. "I was wondering what the story was behind that rock," I said.

Seems that rock had spent the last 75 years or so busting farm equipment in that field up yonder. Like an iceberg, a tip the size of a football belied its true girth

When some excavating was underway nearby a few years back, the opportunity was right. Doc asked the man to tackle the rock. Probably wouldn't cost much.

The man dug. And dug. After a couple hours or so of digging, you might suppose a guy would give it up. But things like that rock become a challenge. An Ahab and Moby Dick sort of thing.

When Doc returned, he had a meteor crater in his field and one surprisingly large rock. "The guy was so proud," Doc remembers. But where to put the monster? Doc favored the hill. Dee wanted it in the flower garden. But when the machine grabbed the stone for transport, the rear wheels rose into the air, helpless.

"So I had to hire a bigger machine to move the rock," Doc continued, chomping on his unlit Dutch Masters cigar.

I grinned and checked my watch.

Before we left, I had to ask the question to which I already suspected the answer. "What can I give you for the cream can?"

"Dee and I talked about it. Most young people don't care about their heritage. The past doesn't mean anything to them... This means something to you. You can have it."

The threads of life are so intricate, I marveled, as I drove home that day. The fibers stretch beyond lifetimes, intertwined in an unrealized pattern.

Doc's father had picked up the can at auction. Who knows how many previous auctions it had survived. And now it was coming home. Dylan's great-great-grandfather had touched us this day.

We had come for an old cream can.

We brought home a memory.

© Tony Bender, 1998

Not from
around here

"Where are you from?" they ask. They know I am not from around here.

They see me glance up at the tall buildings gleaming and marvelous. I do not stare straight ahead like the men in suits and the women in conservative dresses, offering a quick glance but no smile.

Lips tight, stride unbroken, they march on. Time marches on. And me, I'm just watching.

There is an ease to my step, a shuffle, a meander, and that, as much as the micro-camera clinging to my belt, and the fact that I do not have a cell phone pressed to my ear, exposes me as a stranger. A neophyte. A greenhorn. Worse yet, a tourist.

I suppose I am. Maybe. On a technicality, maybe. I had lived in this city long ago, and a piece of me is still here, so I return each year searching for it.

I measure the growth of the city the way the lines scratched into the doorway of a home mark the growth of children. When the lines get high, so high as to astound, the lines stop completely. Eventually, when the residents are a memory and real estate agents have done what they do, some new family will move in and paint over the door jamb without a second thought and begin again.

It is like that in the city. I saw buildings rise when I lived here, and now I see them pushed into cavernous pits by big yellow Caterpillar bulldozers. I own Cat stock. I have always felt it was as noble as stock gets these days. It is a stock optimistic about growth. But growth demands the past be pushed aside, and as I watch the buildings collapse, disposable as a hamburger wrapper, I feel older and dammit, maybe a bit disposable, too.

"North Dakota," I tell the waiter. "We're from North Dakota." He smiles more broadly now, a wonderful grin, and though I know it is not 100 percent sincere, I decide it is at least 90 percent sincere. The more he smiles, the bigger his tip will be, he knows. I know. The Redhead knows. We all know. But we enjoy the smile all the same.

The food is good, the tip big and the smile gigantic as we leave to stroll the darkening streets.

When the young man asks for a quarter, I give him one. Because I am not from around here. I have not yet learned to banish the needy and the crazy from my vision. Not all of them, anyway.

An old man plays Gershwin tunes on a clarinet on the corner beside a box that says "War is Over." I don't think so, but I wish it were true, and now I regret not giving him a dollar because, after all, he was very good. And maybe if I had given, I muse, perhaps the wish would come true. We wish on stars, don't we? Why not on old bald clarinet players? Next year I will give him two dollars if he is still alive.

We do not give to the guitar player because he is badly out of tune, and I quickly deduce that the four chords I know exceed his knowledge of the instrument.

"Where are you from?" I venture in the shuttle to the airport.

"Atlanta," she says. She's from Atlanta via Kansas. Now, she's not in Kansas anymore. She directs "one of those goofy morning TV talk shows."

"Oh. So you're the one that tells the cameraman to zoom in on the omelet," I say.

"That's about it," she says.

When her companion learns we are from North Dakota, he says what everyone says. "It must be cold."

I laugh. "Oh, yes. I can't say that it isn't." And then I tell him how I laugh when Atlanta gets a bit of sleet and they have to shut the city down. "On those days I feel a bit superior."

Then he asks, "So what's in North Dakota?"

I give him the stock answer. The Badlands. Fargo. Lakes and rivers and cowboys and farmers.

"But the best part of it is space. Elbow room," I say. "I really think the prairie is beautiful. I love going for miles and not seeing anyone else. I am a child of the prairie. I love the tall grass prairie. I love the elbow room."

Then I stop, because an answer has turned into a speech and a speech into a sermon, and who wants to hear a sermon on the way to the airport even if it is Sunday?

The talk turns to baseball. That's the big news in Atlanta. "The Braves are really good this year," the director of the goofy morning TV show says with a Kansas twang. "We think they have a good chance of winning the World Series."

"They're always good," I say. "But come October, I'll be pulling for the Twins to win the Series."

She says she understands.

As the two-prop French-made plane lifts off with about 10 of us aboard, I gaze down at the city. I see the precise, small partitions of land, some black where new construction is underway, some green where grass is watered and others brown where the drought has parched the land. From the air, the squares are small, restrictive, almost claustrophobic but so well-planned.

I see the Missouri River as we approach Bismarck. I see the skittering of boats and the splash of skiers.

At first, the partitions of prairie are so vast, even from the air they look as they must have when homesteaders arrived. They look endless, but I know they are not. In this world, in this life, everything is owned and divided.

The partitions get smaller as we get closer to the airport.

More divisions. The fruit of big yellow heavy equipment.

I can see our four wheel drive monstrosity leaning in a way I know it shouldn't lean as we lug our luggage in the August heat. Yup. Tire's flat.

The Redhead suggests we call someone, because I have my nice clothes on and she knows I just hate this sort of thing. Hate it. But I am anxious to get home. So I change the tire.

© Tony Bender, 2002

It means
I'm home

It was the first thing we saw from the windows of that old Chevy station wagon as we approached our new home.

It stood high above the surrounding plains, tall enough to peek over the valley that was a haven for the people of Frederick.

The water tower was green and silver, colors that would have driven city fathers to distraction had their homes been those hues. But for a water tower that proudly bore the name of the town, it must have seemed just right.

That was 1967, and my father had taken a job with the elevator in the only structure to rival the majesty of the tower. We made our home a half a block away from that silver and green giant. Sometimes when I walked to school, I would imagine it falling... Yup, if it fell to the northwest it would just about...

probably fall... right on my bedroom...

Through the years I watched the two strongest arms on my baseball team struggle in vain to hit the tank with mighty throws. I didn't even try when I saw them fall short. In the late summer when Dad was loading boxcars, too busy to watch the games, the tower watched. It saw everything and holds a thousand secrets. It marked every error, every homerun.

On Halloween, pumpkins would mysteriously appear on the catwalk around the tank, peering mockingly down, at all authority. In the spring, declarations like "Class of '72 reigns" would be scrawled on the tower only to be painted out by the next graduates.

One local man, who leased space on the tower for his radio antennae, found out too late that it had been his son who had climbed our Everest to perform some prank. "I could have saved a couple of hundred dollars on installation, had I known that," he groused. I never climbed that tower, though I really wanted to throw a balsa airplane from the peak and watch it stunt its way down. Common sense or fear prevailed.

Through the years, as our gypsy caravan of six kids and Mom and Dad took us to visits to grandparents, it became a contest to spot that city's water tower in the distance. Ashley's, because it was sky blue, was tough to make out some days. And Gackle's snuck up on you. Suddenly the car would top a hill and orange and black steel would appear. No daydreamer ever spotted that tower first.

And there were other towers. We marveled at the huge check-

171

ered abomination in Jamestown. We read the names of smaller towns along the highway from their steel billboards. But being the first to spot the green and silver held the highest honor. It meant we were home.

And even today, as I drive U.S. Highway 281, I find myself scanning the horizon for that tower, and every time it makes me smile just a little bit when I spot it. It means I'm home.

© Tony Bender, 1994

—

✍ PRAIRIE FOLK

Roland was
a big dog

Some days I just don't want to do the job. It's not that I don't love what I do. I do. Most days it comes as natural as breathing.

The thing is, though, when I sit down at this keyboard two hours before the sun even thinks about rising, I have no choice in the matter. I must write what I feel.

Lots of times I write about the glories and humble moments of being an older than average father. I'm sure it gets tiresome for my readers sometimes, but like I said, I have to write what's on my mind if I have any hope of being worth a hoot. The whole ugly truth of the matter is that a writer writes to please himself, but hardly a one of us will admit it.

But you see, I am stalling. I am dancing around the subject now the same way I have danced around it in my head for a couple days. I have tried to drag another topic into my head.

Anything else.

But this thing won't go a way until I complete this exorcism. So I must eulogize. I have done it many times before. It will happen again.

Thing is, when you wade into one of these things, you have to be careful not to build the deceased up beyond what they were in life—at least not beyond what they were in the periphery of your life.

And the thing is, Roland Zimmerman was a Ford dealer. He sold cars—two of them to me. What writer is going to write sentimental tripe about a car dealer? These are guys we all complain about along with lawyers, IRS agents, politicians and the liberal, soulless media.

I get this picture in my head of me walking through life as a smashed-face bull dog. I trot down the street, through life, nodding respectfully at the big dogs I pass. And they nod back. But onward we trot.

Then, when us smaller dogs get together, one of us will mention that the venerable Fido has moved on to the big kennel in the sky after a slip under the wheels of big ass truck. A Ford truck. The best damn truck there is. "He was a big dog," we say. And then we howl at the moon.

I marched into Roland's office my first week in Hettinger as publisher of a newspaper with no advertising.

Maybe you think that newspapers are just one of those inexpensive irritants in your life—that subscriptions pay the freight, and that gives you the right to complain every Wednesday for the rest of your life about typos and ill-informed editorials. The fact is, without advertising there is no newspaper.

Here I was, publisher of an almost bankrupt newspaper, and there, up on the hill was a gleaming Ford dealership with shiny cars. And he wasn't advertising in the local paper.

I shut the door behind me. Roland looked up and frowned at me, the same pained expression I suppose I get when a salesman walks into my office to sell me something I don't want to buy.

"RZ," I announced, "When I leave this office, there's going to be blood on the floor, and your ad is going to be running in my paper."

It happened, too. A quarter page every week for the five years I published the *Adams County Record*.

When I picked up the order each week, he would agonize behind the chair, frowning like he had a toothache. Heavy sighs at good money frittered away.

When The Redhead and I bought cars from him, the frowning escalated, and he would shake his head as he hammered on the calculator, staring incredulously at the numbers. I'm convinced to this day, our outrageous demands forced him to lose thousands on every transaction.

After RZ Motors ads began running in the paper, other businesses followed suit. Roland was a big dog, and if the big dog saw merit in what the newspaper was doing, "well, hey now, we better get with the program."

But before we start getting all warm and sentimental about this tale, remind yourself that I am a newspaperman, and Roland was a car dealer. Snap out of it!

Roland and I weren't best friends, but he was important enough to be a mandatory stop during my visits to Hettinger.

He had stopped frowning—at me at least—probably because there was little chance I would sell him something during these visits.

As I sit here frowning at inadequate words, I have been forced to analyze our friendship. I have been forced to consider why I care about a dead car dealer out among the west river buttes.

My best answer is that it's a simple matter of respect. I admired what he built, and I saw how hard he worked. But even more than that, I understand that the big dogs in this world have the option of snarling and snapping at those they pass. Or they can clear a path for you. That big dog did right by me, and I owe him one.

The funeral is tomorrow.

I'm driving the Mustang.

I shall howl.

© Tony Bender, 2002

He was
a rascal

He was a rascal. And whatever "it" is, he was full of it. That's how I'll remember Reuben.

I stopped by to bring Marlene a hot dish the day before the funeral. I should have brought her another refrigerator from the looks of the overflow of food chilling in the garage.

Rodney was there and on the table were photos of Reuben and that gap-tooth grin that had demanded we grin back so many times.

There were pictures of Reuben with his grandchildren and in those pictures, the grin was a little wider. Even as he lay at home in his deathbed, he would hear a scuffle break out in the basement between Rodney's boys, and Reuben would smile a sort of satisfied smile. "It was music to his ears," Rodney said.

179

Reuben loved a ruckus. Lived for anarchy. He loved to tease and he was a big flirt.

There were pictures of Reuben as a dapper young soldier in the early 1950s. Reuben had met Marlene at a dance about that time. "He was verrrrry charming," Marlene smiled.

"He had to be to get a girl like you, Marlene," I said, because it's the truth.

And there was a picture of Reuben proudly astride a gleaming black wild stallion he had broken. I laughed at the irony. One wild stallion attempting to tame another.

"I would see him walking down the street, and he would be limping," Pastor Stahl remembered at the funeral, "or he would be holding his arm. And I would ask him, 'Reuben, what happened?'"

Of course the damage had been inflicted by the stallion.

"I had to wait until Marlene left the house to get out of bed, so she wouldn't see me limping," Reuben told Pastor Stahl.

As I sipped my coffee, I remembered riding with Reuben on his creamery route. And when he spotted a young rabbit in a field, we would stop and Reuben, in his forties, wearing boots, would run down rabbits for us to keep as pets.

"There were lots and lots of rabbits," Rodney remembered. "One time he caught a fox. He got mad at me for letting it loose in town."

Reuben never stopped being a kid. And when we were kids, he didn't just revel in our escapades. He was an instigator. Once he put out a contract on a neighborhood tuffie. He promised us a quarter if we'd rough him up a bit—a formidable task—so we promised the bully a nickel to take the fall.

I always felt I had kind of a special relationship with Reuben. But after listening to the stories told around town after he died, it was clear he made everyone feel that way. "I could always count on Reuben," one old friend said. "When I needed help, Reuben was always there," said another.

"He worked hard," Rodney agreed, shaking his head slowly at the memories.

When Rodney took up golf last summer, it puzzled Reuben. He'd drive up and catch us on the Par 3 by the school and Rodney would roll his eyes.

"He just didn't understand us chasing that little ball around when there was work to be done," Rodney said.

"If I could, I'd tell him, 'Reuben, I didn't understand a lot of the things you did either,'" I chuckled.

I'm going to miss that old rascal. I'll miss the grin. The easy way he leaned over to tell an anecdote.

As The Redhead carried Dylan past the casket, the boy wondered, "Why is Reuben in a treasure chest?"

"Because he's a treasure," she answered.

© Tony Bender, 2000

Kind of
a drag

I didn't know someone had been stealing gas from Gib Rajha's immaculate farm a mile east of Frederick. I had no idea.

Sunny Pence didn't know. Curt Christianson sure didn't know. Otherwise, I'm sure we could have found a better place to drag race.

Sunny had a '68 gold Camaro, 327 short block, Cherry Bomb mufflers, jacked up back end with mag wheels. He had painted the hubs glow-in-the-dark lime green.

I still think that's wrong.

Curt's 1967 gray Pontiac Catalina was stock with a respectable 400 cubic inches under the hood.

After Sunny came back from the service, he made it a point to race virtually anything that moved. There wasn't a John Deere that could touch him—not off the line, anyway.

And I'm not going to suggest that the shredded transmission in my parents' 1967 Chevy station wagon with the 396 and four barrel carb had anything at all to do with drag racing because I'm not sure what the statute of limitations is on something like that.

It was winter. I don't remember the rest of circumstances—because of age, mind you, and not because there was any beer drinking involved. Those things weren't done back then. In fact, beer wasn't even invented yet.

As a passenger in Curt's car, I was the starter. We lined up with Sunny in the right lane, Curt in the left, on a flat stretch of highway heading east toward Hecla.

We lined up at Rajha's east approach—not far from the gas tanks, I guess, revving engines, discussing the rules of engagement.

Suddenly, Sunny took off. I thought he was cheating. Then I looked behind me to see a red 1972 four-wheel drive Ford pickup sliding sideways, tires smoking, out of the west approach that led to the Rajha house.

I should tell you a little about Gib Rajha. There wasn't a nicer, more dignified family around. Dignified is the key word. If Gib wasn't a deacon of St. Paul's Lutheran Church, he should have been.

Anyway, by the time Curt developed a plan, which consisted of sheer panic and hitting the accelerator, I was staring up into the window of a Ford pickup as we careened down the highway, where a madman in a bathrobe was shifting gears like Mario Andretti.

At this juncture, let me say that if you have a 1967 Catalina and you have the inclination to race a '72 Ford pickup, don't bother.

You gonna lose.

Then, as the nose of the pickup lurched ahead, the driver did the most amazing thing. He started ramming the side of the Pontiac where I was sitting, me looking up in terror without a bottle of beer in my hand, him looking down at me in a very nicely fitted pair of pajamas and plaid robe. I don't remember for sure, but in my mind I think "Little Old Lady From Pasadena" was on the radio.

I don't mind telling you, this is not the way drag racing is supposed to work.

I don't recall our conversation—it may have involved a shucks or a by golly—but I remember Curt's eyes. They were wide open like we were gonna die.

When the pickup finally rammed us into a snowbank in the ditch, the driver stopped. I watched as a fifty-year-old man in pajamas waded through three feet of snow to the passenger side door where I was sitting without a bottle of Schlitz in my hand.

When he got there, I rolled down the window as casually as if we had stopped on Frederick's two block main street to chat with a buddy. When you have just been run off the road by a man in pajamas who has just invented road rage, you are real interested in what he has to say.

184

I cranked down the window, Gib's eyes got big and mine did, too, when I recognized him. I had never pegged him for a mad-man, and he had never suspected me of being a gas thief.

After I had explained that we were drag racing and not steal-ing gas, Gib turned red—it must have been the cold—and he drove back to get a tractor and a chain to pull us out. I think he changed out of his pajamas.

It was real cool to see Gib the next morning in church. His wife and two kids grinned wide perfect grins and tried to stifle laughter. Gib was still red.

If anyone has a better Gib Rajha story, I'd sure like to hear it.

© Tony Bender, 2002

Writer's note: I ran into Gib the other day. He said I got it all wrong. He never even owned a plaid robe, he said. He didn't deny the rest of the stuff, though.

✍ RELATIVELY SPEAKING

Day of the Locust

I fidget. I will fidget at every church service for the rest of my life except for my funeral. Today will be worse. I study the numbers on the bank clocks as we go through town. Each one records a temperature in excess of 100 degrees. It is 108 in Bismarck. I am certain I am going to witness the death of an old codger at this wedding.

Locust has chosen the family farm as the site for her wedding. She is making The Redhead wear a hot long dark purple bridesmaid dress, vengeance for all the times she was mean to her. (She used to feed live bugs to the baby, so Laura became Locust.)

The bridesmaids look like a cluster of grapes. Sweaty grapes. They are holding Locust's dress high above her ankles so what little breeze there is can dry the sweat on her legs.

189

She threw up in the living room, but it had nothing whatsoever to do with the keg of beer in the machine shed last night, mind you. It's the heat. The heat and nerves.

There are two preachers. Just in case one keels over with heat stroke.

I am taking pictures, because I am a newspaperman, and I have a camera, and I am the closest thing there is in the family to a professional. But they've hired another semi-professional. Just in case. We each believe the other is the backup.

As the Redhead walks by on the arm of another man, it bothers me. A little.

"You got a new squeeze?" I ask.

"Yes," she says maliciously. "He's tall."

I am not. If she is not wearing heels, I come up to her chest. Which is not all bad. If she is wearing heels, we have to wire warning beacons to her head so low-flying planes do not bump into her.

Her escort is the groom's brother, Jeff. He is from Michigan.

"So what do you do in Wisconsin?" I ask.

"Michigan," he says.

"Same thing," I say.

He works for Upjohn. They make pharmaceuticals. The good thing about selling drugs in a down economy is that people continue to spend money on them, he tells me. They make Rogaine. Even in the Great Depression, as I recall from my history lessons, people were intensely concerned about their hair.

"But now," he says, "we're being sued by the federal government. They think we're charging too much."

"You probably are," Eric says.

"We probably are," Jeff says.

When the DJ announces it is time for the wedding party to dance, they rush to the floor because they hear the word "party."

So I lose The Redhead to the tall guy. They look good together on the dance floor, a concrete slab outside the golf course clubhouse. It irritates me, but I snap some photos (out of focus) just to show I am a good sport.

The tall pharmaceutical man's wife is snapping pictures, too.

"My baby's first prom!" she says.

While our spouses are dancing, I chat her up.

She is a professional psychic, she tells me.

"Me, too," I say, holding my fingers to my temple in deep concentration. "The spirits tell me you are from Wisconsin."

"Michigan," she says.

Stupid spirits.

She is spectacular, this psychic, a hot tamale poured into an orange dress. In fact, she is overflowing, if you know what I mean. She has black hair and a naughty smile when she dances.

She's about my height.

"Are you hustling Jeff's wife?" The Redhead asks when the dance is over.

"Of course," I say.

"You might as well," Jeff says. "Everyone else does."

"Were you looking at my chest?" the psychic asks with a

wicked little grin. She doesn't use the word chest, but you know what I mean. Because she is psychic, I cannot lie.

The DJ, whose name is Dude, and that in itself is very cool, is having problems. The breaker keeps knocking him off line. After the third time, he throws his arms into the air.

I look up. It is growing dark in the west, and it is not just the night. It looks like rain.

I promise to dance with The Redhead but never really get around to it. But I do dance with the bride. For a buck. Someone cuts in after two verses.

The Redhead kisses me and sings along badly to *"Paradise by the Dashboard Light."* She gets a glint in her eye when she sings *"We were barely 17 and we were barely dressed."*

I am sitting on the concrete step when Dude plays a special slow song. It is their song. It must be. Locust wraps her perfectly manicured hands around Eric's neck, lightly caressing, and she looks into his eyes, and he looks into hers. He is wearing sandals.

We all disappear. The shrieking children rolling down the perfectly mowed fairway are gone. The crowds buzzing around the dance floor, the mothers scanning the crowd for their youngsters, the waitress picking up empties, they all vanish. Dude is gone. There is just the music, a song I cannot remember because it is not my song.

Two dancers sway slowly. The sky flashes in the west, but it does not rain.

© Tony Bender, 2002

4.5 on the
dead cat scale

You try to keep her happy. Contrary to popular perception, men do try to keep their wives happy.

We make all sorts of concessions. We start changing our underwear almost daily. We stop drinking beer on the way to church. We make apologetic behavior a high art, complete with bowing and scraping and "Yes, Dears" galore. We try.

But when a woman starts messing with a man's stereo system, it could be a deal-breaker.

The Redhead complained bitterly about the giant old Kenwood speakers designed by the famous speaker engineer Ken Wood from actual California Redwood stumps in 1974.

But it seems they interfered with The Redhead's decorating. "They are so not Feng Shui!" So she tried to hide them. First behind furniture and then in DeLane Dollinger's pasture.

I was patient. "Honey, you can't put stuff in front of the speakers."

"Why not?"

"Then you can't hear them."

"Sooo?"

Now, I'm not going to say that she actually forced me to sell my speakers, but like I said, a guy tries to keep his wife happy.

Plus, I figured I could slip a new DVD player into the mix without her noticing. I auditioned a fabulous sounding system. Five speakers, DVD player—the whole sha-bang—a sha-bang with extremely low total harmonic convergence, to be precise.

Then I did something really stupid. I ordered the system off the Internet as my Father's Day gift to myself (because I had been very, very good). I got exactly what I ordered. Dummy.

But I didn't set it up until last week. That's when I discovered I had ordered the 300 Sony Dream System as opposed to the 700 series I had auditioned. I guess that's why I got such a great deal.

So now, in a room slightly larger than Wind Cave, I had a system spectacularly engineered for my bedroom.

I listened to it for two days trying to convince myself I had done the right thing. I played *The Matrix* which is to DVD what *Dark Side of the Moon* is to CD.

The sound was incredible, but in order to achieve the effect I wanted, I had to use bungy cords to mount the speakers on my head. I duct-taped the sub-woofer to my leg, and it was great

194

but not at all convenient. And it frightened the children.

Now, for your average guy, it's a great system. But for a guy who used to choose roommates strictly on the basis of their stereo equipment, ignoring other criteria like whether they bathed, drank from the milk carton or cleaned the bong, this would not do.

Unfortunately, I had already sold my speakers. I got lots of calls after the ad ran. One local farmer wanted just one speaker to convert into a lambing barn. But he wondered if it would cost too much to heat, and then when I refused to break up the set, he backed out of the deal, complaining bitterly that even when the niblets are priced 3/$2 at Super Valu, he still gets the sale price even if he buys only one can.

Eventually the speakers were purchased by Bobby Delzer, who collects speakers the way Mariah Carey collects psychoses. I gave him a pretty good deal because he was depressed about the death of his cat, Fluffy. Poor thing wandered too close to a 12 inch subwoofer during a Metallica drum solo. Fluffy will be sorely missed.

I'm sure the trauma caused by the loss of my speakers was not lost on The Redhead. She tried to umm... ahh... cheer me up, but I just couldn't. "I just don't feel like a real man anymore."

So faced with living with a man whose testosterone levels were plummeting dangerously close to Richard Simmons territory, she suggested I go speaker shopping the next day.

I auditioned nine sets of speakers. Most guys don't date that many girls before deciding to propose.

I really liked one set, but this was a really big decision... I hemmed and hawed until I paged through the brochure and discovered they had been endorsed by Bobby Delzer. He rated them 4 and 1/2 dead cats on a five cat scale.

Of course at home, I soon discovered that my twelve year old stereo was not up to the task of pushing the speakers. Plus, it could only process the old Pro Logic surround sound format and not the superior (the salesman said) Dolby Digital format of the new DVDs. Well, you know what happened. Now I have a system which handles the new DVD format and is so loud it knocked loose a blockage in my left ventricle.

I also have a new remote control so sophisticated, I will have to go back to college to learn how to use it.

Or maybe, if the Redhead doesn't mind, maybe I could room with Bobby.

© Tony Bender, 2002

Borrowing Matthew

We borrowed Matthew Kretschmar twice over Christmas vacation because vacation for children is no vacation for parents.

I love my son, and I dutifully followed him to his room, oh, about 600 times in a two day stretch, to witness the marvelous things he could do with educational software. He's learning new languages—why I do not know. He hasn't even mastered the basics of English yet. Simple stuff like "Yes, Father. I will clean up my room."

So, exhausted, and let's be honest here, looking forward to sluffing a bit, I dialed the the number I have now committed to memory. To let you know what a big deal that is—that I memorized a phone number—I recently had to leave my home number on voice mail, and under the pressure of the tape rolling, I couldn't remember it.

I'm sure the folks at the restaurant, at which I was making reservations, had a real big laugh over that. They'll probably put crayons beside my salad fork when we get there. But I won't forget Matthew's number. It's like remembering 911.

Dave, Matthew's dad, did not argue when I proposed borrowing Matthew, because halfway through Christmas vacation, he was exhausted from the Gameboy marathon. He even delivered Matthew to our home 12 miles out in the country.

It was a brilliant stroke. They played beautifully together, cleaned up their messes and did not complain about the lunch menu.

Then, Matthew did something we had never seen before. He carried his plate to the sink. Volunteered. Right out of the clear blue.

My creamed corn went down the wrong way, and I started choking. Then something even more fantastic happened. Dylan carried his plate over, too.

The Redhead gasped, and pointed, speechless, as incredulous as the time she was convinced she'd spotted a Dodo bird in the pasture across the road.

On Saturday, I borrowed Matthew again, and again solitude and good behavior were the order of the day. In the silence I swear I heard the faint chorus of "Peace in the Valley."

By this weekend, the Kretschmars wanted some of this action. After his return to school, Dylan had been reinvigorated with precocious energy, so I was willing.

The plan was for Dylan to ride the bus to Kretschmar's after school on Friday. Dylan would spend the night, so I dropped off his suitcase with Dave, who was watching the newest of four dogs so small, together they add up to half a German Shepherd, do his business in the snow.

After the morning's argument over breakfast cereal, the loss of his mittens and what is 9 plus 9—it is 99 isn't it—I was thrilled at the prospect of some silence.

"What time Saturday do you want to pick up Dylan?" Dave asked, holding a steaming mug of coffee as the pug sniffed about.

"Sunday," I said.

Things were going so well, Lori called to say she wondered if Dylan could stay another day.

"Does he have enough clothes?"

"He can wear Matthew's."

He and Matthew are just about the same size. They even look alike—two little cherubic tow heads. At school, it wears on Dylan that he is mistaken for Matthew, but as long as he keeps getting Matthew's test scores, he's willing to ride it out.

"I have to tell you something," Lori confided, lowering her voice. "Dylan has been sooo polite and after dinner, he carried his plate to the sink. That's never happened around here!"

Yesterday morning, when I arrived to pick him up, Dylan pleaded to stay two more days. Not one more day, but two, because he's part German and therefore already instinctively astute at the process of negotiation.

"I'm sorry, Dylan. But if you stay two more days, you will officially become a Kretschmar. It's the law. I'm OK with that, but I think your mother would be upset."

He groused for the first five miles until I offered to take the discussion outside—it has happened.

So he sulked. When we walked in the door to the prison that has become his home, his mother greeted him with outstretched arms. He stared. And then he walked to his room and closed the door.

I'm calling Matthew. And, no, you can't have the number.

© Tony Bender, 2002

It will
be all right

Finally, I am fixing the boy's computer. It's been weeks since he has been able to use it without it locking up. But I have an hour before the movie starts, and the babysitter is already here. I shall make good use of the time.

This would make it two weekends in a row that we go out to see a movie. That's never happened. Not even when we didn't have children, did we make it to the movies two weekends in a row.

Then I hear it. The screech has an unusual pitch. I sit. I listen. There is a fine line between celebration and fear, between a joyous screech and the screech of fear.

I was spending a few weeks at my grandparents' farm as I did every summer when I was younger, in idler times. I was sprawled inches from the morning television... *I Love Lucy* reruns, I think, when I heard what sounded like laughter in the kitchen.

My grandmother had a big happy laugh and this sound, whatever it was, was big. I stood and walked to the kitchen where Grandma stood with my aunt.

"What's so funny?" I wondered. Then I learned that my great-grandmother had died. Yes, there is a fine line between exaltation and mourning.

I listen closer to the scream, tuning in. Then I am certain. And I am relieved. A scream means he is alive.

His mother is cradling him at the foot of the stairs, blood pouring from his head, and it is chaos.

Baby India chases the cat. The babysitter watches, eyes wide.

The Redhead's white sweatshirt is turning crimson, and she wants to know what happened, but the boy is too excited by all the blood to produce a cognitive answer.

The Redhead rushes for two washcloths as I slap my palm over the gushing wound. It does little good. I can feel the warm, wet red stuff flowing between my fingers and drip, drip, dripping onto the growing crimson ring on his yellow hockey jersey.

"It's going to be all right," I tell him and I know it will be.

The babysitter calls the doctor while the washcloths are applied. I skip down the stairs to rinse the blood from my hands and to see what accident caused this tumult.

A 30 pound speaker lies beside the pedestal, beside the aquarium, where he is forbidden to go. And now he knows why.

For a moment, I wonder if the speaker is damaged. Then I stop fretting. My son's head has broken the fall.

This will be our third trip to the emergency room this month. India was in twice with a rotovirus.

They are so competitive.

I do not speed. He is calmer now and angry about my speaker placement. "It will be all right," I smile.

He balks at the idea of stitches. He just wants to go home. The last time he had stitches, he was only three and the daycare provider panicked. So he panicked, and they wrapped him in a sheet while they stitched the knee. And now those memories return two years later. *It hurt.*

This time it won't. Not much, at least, we say. Finally, after hugs and assurances, he bravely lies down and we are proud.

"Did you know, Dylan, that this is the hospital where I had my first stitches?" He listens. That was in 1959—eight stitches.

It is not the worst wound the doctor has stitched today. Just seven quick stitches, some paperwork, and the drive-in beckons.

We will bring ice cream home. Two pints. One vanilla, one chocolate. Soft serve.

The boy chatters happily. That makes 11 stitches total. He's averaging better than two a year.

The Redhead serves the ice cream, and she looks at me knowingly above the clatter of the spoons.

In moments like these, as the ice cream spots the carpet, and the din rises, we smile and remember meeting for the first time, and we shake our heads at how that has led to this.

"Hey, Dad, the computer works again! Thanks, Dad!"

The movie has already started, but we have a babysitter so we might as well go back to town. We'll find something to do.

Everything's gonna be all right.

© Tony Bender, 2002

Love letters
from Mom

I ndia was up at 2 a.m. She'd managed to tear the corner off her diaper and well...you know what happened. I didn't have to get up, and The Redhead didn't actually blame me; even though, I was the one who changed her before bedtime, but still it was sleep lost. So I am up at 5:45 a.m. to write my column instead of the usual 5 a.m.

At 6 a.m., Dylan stumbled into my office, still in a sleepy trance. Of course, I booted him out. I may have to institute the "Don't Interrupt Dad Until 7:30 Rule."

It's ironic, I know, that so often in this place I write about our moments together, but to do it, I must be alone.

But, like I said, I am running late this morning. Dylan must be at school at 8 a.m. so the luxury I used to have of just getting to work a bit later is gone. Deadlines loom.

205

In desperation sometimes, I dredge up an old column and send it out. Recycling is very popular nowadays.

This morning, I stumbled upon a column from 1993. Before The Redhead. Before Dylan. Before India. Before my life changed in a most marvelous way. I want to share some excerpts.

I don't know if mothers put together baby books anymore or if that custom has been lost in these times of working moms. If that's the case so much is being lost. On a whim, I picked up my fading satin baby book and delved in I wasn't prepared for the discovery. I know so very well who I am now, but I really had no idea who I was...

In 1959 my parents had just moved from a small basement apartment to a four room house. I was one. My 20-year-old mother entered this in the journal: *"At first you didn't know what to think of all the room, Tony. But the second day you began exploring every room of your new home. I believe you must have lost weight for all the running you did!*

"You did something that is funny now, but at the time, when your mother was so tired and ready to drop, you found a nice 12 ounce bottle of olive oil in one of the boxes.

"And how you ever got it open, I didn't know. Anyway, Daddy and Mother were busy in the other rooms trying to get things unpacked when I realized it was altogether too quiet and went to see where you were...

"There you sat in the middle of a huge olive oil puddle in the kitchen. You were just dripping with the stuff but didn't seem to

206

mind as you were busily rubbing it all over the floor and on your hands. Mommy was so angry!

"And when you heard her yell at you, you tried to get up and run away but fell because the floor was so slippery. You tried again; fell again. The third time you did get out of the mess and Mommy started wiping up the oil after patting your butt a couple of times.

"When I was through with the wiping up of the oil in the kitchen, I looked around and there were little olive oil footprints throughout the house. They stayed there too, until the next day, when after a good night's sleep, I cleaned them up, too. See how helpful you were?"

"That Saturday you spilled most of the furniture polish on the end table, too. But I suppose that was my fault for leaving it within your reach. But little boys can't grow up without doing a few things they shouldn't can they?"

I got a lump in my throat as I read the lines. As I read further in the baby book I see the shiny black and white picture of the pouty boy and his pretty sister next to the Christmas tree. It was 1964. The family had grown. I had, too.

"You wondered if Grandpa and Grandma liked the gloves and mittens you and Sherry and Pat and Scott had bought for them," my mother wrote.

"You're beginning to think of giving instead of just getting gifts and we're very pleased...

"You bought your mother a pretty dish—went uptown alone and picked it out by yourself, and you were so proud! And it was

Mom's favorite gift, too."

And back to today. Dylan has stomped back upstairs after his unkind expulsion, and here I sit listening to the racket the two kids are making—because he woke India up, too. I read the lines my mother wrote through misty eyes.

We have not done a very good job with our children's baby books. But we stash memorabilia away for them in giant trunks. And I sit here and write my own letters of love knowing full well they will sit some morning with their coffee cooling and read them.

They will cry, too, and know how much I love them. Now, I suppose I must apologize to Dylan and listen... India is calling my name... "Da-Da! Da-Da!"

She is right outside the door. I guess I'm done.

© Tony Bender, 2002 (1993)

About
the author

Tony Bender gained national recognition in 2001 when he was awarded a first place prize for humor writing by the National Newspaper Association for his piece entitled, *The Redhead's*

Tractor, which is contained in his first collection of writing, *Loons in the Kitchen.* Bender won the award again in 2002 with *Reasonably Functional for a Moron,* a piece included in this book. He earned seven first place newspaper association awards for his column in the '90s.

Bender began publishing his weekly syndicated column, *"That's Life,"* in 1991, writing for his hometown paper, the *Brown County News* in Frederick, SD. That very first year, Bender scored a first place award for his column in the South Dakota Newspaper Association's annual contest.

Born in 1958 in Ashley, ND, Bender grew up in Frederick, a tiny community on the North Dakota-South Dakota border, 26 miles north of Aberdeen, SD. That community with a population of 400 provided Bender with a "Tom Sawyer existence" that surfaces in his writing as he tells the tales of the characters he grew to love.

After a year of journalism at South Dakota State University in Brookings, SD, Bender, in 1977, opted for hands-on experience and embarked on a radio career including stops at KSDN and KKAA in Aberdeen and KQDJ in Jamestown, ND. In 1983, Bender moved to Denver where he worked at KHOW and KIMN.

His sense of adventure took him to Juneau, AK in 1986, where he starred at KTKU with his unique morning show featuring alter-egos like obnoxious newsman Irving R. Osgood and the unscrupulous Rev. Billy Joe Jim-Bob. In 1988, Bender was awarded the *"Goldie,"* a top honor from the Alaska Radio and Television Association, for his accomplishments at KTKU.

In 1989, Bender accepted a morning drive position at WBPR in Myrtle Beach, SC. Shortly after his arrival, Hurricane Hugo struck. While all other broadcast stations evacuated, Bender and his newsman elected to stay to broadcast to the many listeners who had not been able to evacuate in time. As the only station on the air for hundreds of miles delivering crucial information, the effort was widely applauded by South Carolina officials and citizens.

In 1990, Bender returned to North Dakota to be closer to his family, accepting a position as news director at KYYY, Bismarck. In 1991, he took a position as a reporter at the *Williston Daily Herald*. Six months later he was offered the publishership of the floundering *Adams County Record* in Hettinger, ND.

Bender sparked a resurgence in the *Adams County Record* leading it to two *General Excellence Awards*, the highest honor from the North Dakota Newspaper Association. He served as executive news director for the parent company, Dickson Media, until 1997.

Bender was presented the first-ever *North Dakota Newspaper Association First Amendment Award* in 2000. Bender led the *Ashley Tribune* to NDNA Sweepstakes Awards in 2000 and 2001. He is a two-time winner of the *North Dakota Heritage Writing Contest.* His writing has been published in *North Dakota Outdoors, The National Newspaper Association's Publishers Auxiliary, The Journal of Indian Wars* and newspapers in many states.

Bender has published two previous collections of his work, *Loons in the Kitchen* (2000) and *The Great and Mighty Da-Da* (2001). His column has an estimated readership of 100,000 each week.

Bender and his wife, Julie, have two children, Dylan and India, and reside in rural McIntosh County in North Dakota.

Get the Tony Bender trilogy... Autographed...

ORDER TOLL FREE • 1-877-566-2665 • Visa/MC • $19.95 per book (includes shipping)

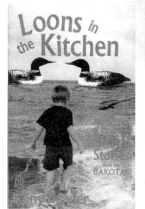
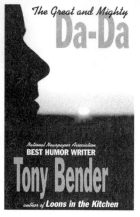

R E D H E A D

PUBLISHING, INC.

☐ **THE GREAT AND MIGHTY DA-DA** (signed copy)
☐ **LOONS IN THE KITCHEN** (signed copy)
☐ **PRAIRIE BEAT** (signed copy)
Check box for each book ordered. Mail $21.95 for each book ordered to Redhead Publishing, P.O. 178, Ashley, ND, 58413.

Name_____

Address_____

City_____ State_____ Zip_____

Also from Redhead Publishing...

L. Gale Johnson's Barefoot Down the Cowpath!

Available on amazon.com and from Redhead Publishing, Box
178, Ashley, ND 58413. Send $19.95 (includes shipping).
www.ashleynd.com/barefoot

212